Amy Carmichael

Amy Carmichael

by
Fern Neal Stocker

A Guessing Book

MOODY PRESS
CHICAGO

ISBN: 0-8024-4760-0

1 2 3 4 5 6 7 Printing/LC/Year 92 91 90 89 88 87

Printed in the United States of America

To my daughter
Polly,
who, like Amy Carmichael, never gives in to difficulty

Contents

To You, the Reader:

A Guessing Book is the story of a famous person. As you read along in this Guessing Book, you'll come to questions you can answer by yourself.

One, two, or three guesses are given, and you can choose one, two, or three answers. Sometimes all are correct, sometimes none. (You'll find the answer as you keep reading.) Pretty soon you'll know the person in the story so well you can get the answer right every time.

It may be fun to keep track of how many guesses you get right. But if you miss one, don't worry—this isn't a test.

Read this Guessing Book and learn about Amy Carmichael, a woman who followed God's plan for her life.

1

Homesick

"**B**ut I don't want to go to school in England!" Amy Carmichael glared at her two younger brothers.

"Don't blame us!" Ernest said. "It's your own fault."

"How can you say that?"

"Oh, I suppose you don't know!" Davy jeered. "I suppose you can't remember running off most all the tutors—except Miss Milne!"

Amy was silent.

"And," Ernest went on, "you know you spent your school time last year teaching Ethel and Ava instead of doing your own work."

"You did everything but your own lessons," Davy pursued. "Miss Milne couldn't get you to

GUESS	1. do a single math problem." 2. water the flowers." 3. read any books."

Amy knew she had not done her math problems.

"But I love Ireland. Why do I have to go to school in England?" she asked.

"Mother told you a hundred times that's what would happen if you didn't change your ways."

"And you didn't!"

"But I never thought she'd really send me away." Amy's clothes were packed. Her trunk stood on the porch waiting for the carriage to come.

But Amy still didn't really believe

GUESS	1. Mother was sick.
	2. she was going.
	3. she was flying.

Amy still didn't believe she was going, even when she heard her mother call upstairs, "Come, Amy, it's time."

Dragging her feet, Amy went down the steps. She squeezed back the tears and clung to the bannister to keep from falling.

At the foot of the stairs, Mother took her in her arms. "Amy, dear, it's not the end of the world. I was eleven, just like you, when I went off to this same school." Mother choked, dabbed her eyes, and patted Amy on the head. She said,

GUESS	1. "You'll meet boys."
	2. "You'll make friends."
	3. "You'll have fun."

"Friends!" Disbelief filled Amy's eyes. "I'll go, but I'll never like those English girls."

"If you are looking for a perfect friend, you'll never have any friends, my dear." Mother pulled Amy out to the wide veranda.

"Father's coming with the carriage," Ethel called. Then she ran and threw her arms around her sister, while little Ava clutched her legs.

"Here, you sillies, let me kiss you a proper good-bye. I can't go if you hold me so."

Ava begged,

1. "Try to like your new school."

12

| GUESS | 2. "Have fun."
| | 3. "Don't go!"

In spite of Ava's crying, "Don't go!" Amy managed to get into the carriage with Father. The coachman loaded her trunk on top of the carriage. Then he jumped up onto the front seat to drive the horses.

She looked back as the driver clucked to the horses, and the carriage began to move. There stood her dear family, waving on the pillared veranda of the gray stone mansion. The carriage completed the circle in front of the house and proceeded down the tree-lined driveway to the main road along the seacoast.

Father broke the silence. "Amy, you know we do this for your own good. We love you, so it hurts us to have you go. Our home here is not the whole world, as you seem to think."

"And Harrogate is?" Amy cried tearfully.

"No, of course not, but this adventure will help you. I would never let you go if I didn't believe that." Father turned to hide the tears in his own eyes.

Suddenly Amy said, "Then you are not punishing me for

| GUESS | 1. leading the boys on the top of the seawall?"
| | 2. walking on the edge of the roof?"
| | 3. almost getting lost at sea?"

"Oh, Amy, is that what you think?" Father gasped. "Of course you should not have done all those things, but going away to school is not punishment. No, oh, no, dear—we want you to get an education. I'll be looking for good reports from Miss Kay."

Amy looked at him. She said,

| GUESS | 1. "I won't like it."
| | 2. "I'll do my best."
| | 3. "You'll be proud."

Amy said, "I'll do my best."

She traveled by ship to England and then by train to Harrogate.

13

By now Amy actually looked forward to seeing where she would be living.

But compared to the Carmichael home in Ireland, the gray walls of Marborough House seemed dreary. At first Amy spoke little, while her sharp eyes saw much. To her the girls in their uniforms all looked alike.

Amy's bed was third in a long line of cots. Near it was a little wash stand and a small wardrobe. Soon she was answering bells for meals, bells for classes, bells for play, bells for study, and bells for bedtime. She wrote home, "It's not as bad as I expected, but everyone talks funny—very English!"

One day the morning bell rang. Amy hurried down the hall, late as usual. She stumbled outside and rushed toward the dining room for breakfast. Outside the door she noticed a pail of rainwater under a downspout. In the pail

> GUESS

1. a mouse struggled.
2. tadpoles played.
3. goldfish swam.

A mouse frantically struggled in the water. "Oh, you poor thing," Amy exclaimed. She swept him up with her hand. Then she stepped inside, found her place at the nearest corner table, and quietly hid the mouse under her full skirt.

The mouse

> GUESS

1. squirmed.
2. got away.
3. squeaked.

Everyone looked her way when they heard a squeak, but Amy looked so innocent they turned their attention back to the man who was giving a Bible talk. All through the speech, squeaking noises came from Amy's corner. The other girls at her table looked uncomfortable, but none blushed so pink as Amy.

She quivered when the mouse

GUESS	1. tore her dress.
	2. bit her finger.
	3. jumped.

Amy controlled herself when the mouse bit her finger, but the blood stained her skirt. In the quiet dining hall, a hundred girls listened. When the speaker said it was time for prayer, Amy held her breath. Surely the mouse would be quiet. But he wasn't! "Squeak, squeak, squeak," he protested, trying to get away.

Amy saw Miss Kay, the director of the school, excuse herself from her table and come toward Amy's corner.

She whispered, "What is wrong?"

All the girls gaped.

"I said, 'What's wrong?' Who is causing a commotion?" She examined the faces of the girls and then set her eye on

GUESS	1. Elizabeth.
	2. Mary.
	3. Amy.

Miss Kay looked directly into Amy's brown eyes. "Were you squealing?"

"No, Mum," Amy replied.

Just then the mouse gave a jerk and a loud squeak. Miss Kay moved to Amy's side, saw the bloodstain, and lifted the fold of Amy's dress. Amy held the mouse to her heart.

"Eek! Eek!" Miss Kay cried, rushing across the room. "A mouse, a mouse!"

The girls screamed, ran, and jumped up and down like yoyos. Amy

GUESS	1. also screamed.
	2. let the mouse go.
	3. sat still.

Bewildered, Amy sat still. Finally the speaker himself grasped

"Eek! Eek!" Miss Kay cried.

her by the shoulders, pulled her to her feet, led her to the yard, and ordered, "Let the mouse go!"

Amy let the little animal run happily

| GUESS | 1. into the schoolroom.
2. up the man's pant leg.
3. into the fields. |

Amy sighed as the mouse ran into a nearby field. Everyone returned to the dining room and ate a cold breakfast. Amy overheard someone say,

| GUESS | 1. "She's crazy."
2. "She's wild."
3. "She's Irish." |

The English girls laughed. "Did you see Miss Kay run from that crazy Irish girl?" they asked each other. "Miss Kay, always so proper. Did you see her face?"

"You do have nerve!" They grinned at Amy across the table. "But you'll catch a bit of trouble, no doubt."

Amy saw the inside of Miss Kay's office often during the coming months. During the years 1881 and 1882 she tried to be good, with little success. Even during her third year she was almost

| GUESS | 1. sent home in disgrace.
2. without friends.
3. displeasing to Father. |

Many times Amy thought she would be sent home, like the time she wanted to see the

| GUESS | 1. comet.
2. circus.
3. snake. |

"You girls must sleep," Miss Kay said. But Amy whispered to her special friends, "I've figured out a way to see the comet anyway." And she told them her plan.

First Amy tied

GUESS

1. a rope to a tall pole.
2. a string around their big toes.
3. Miss Kay's hands together.

When the girls were in bed, Amy tied a string to a toe of each friend. Then she stayed awake and waited. When the time seemed right, she pulled the strings. And the girls woke up. "Come," Amy whispered. And they all silently slipped up the stairway to the attic.

But what a surprise! In the attic they found

GUESS

1. the comet.
2. the teachers.
3. the cat.

There were all the teachers gazing out the window at the comet. Miss Kay looked at them and sighed. "You may as well take a look at the comet since you are here." Amy

GUESS

1. fainted.
2. was sent home.
3. didn't care.

Amy crept down the long hall to Miss Kay's office the next day. "Oh, don't expel me," she begged, trembling. "Father would be so disappointed."

Miss Kay shook her head. "Why did you not think of that before you acted?" After a long pause, she said, "As punishment, you cannot go to the spring picnic."

"Thank you," Amy said and fled to tell her friends.

Amy managed to stay out of trouble for the next few weeks. By

18

now she was looking forward to graduation and going home at last.

"Just think!" Mary exclaimed. "We are down to the last event of the year—then graduation!"

"And home!" Amy added. "What is the last event, anyway? I'm so tired of studying, I could scream."

"Don't you know?" Mary asked. "Everyone is talking about the Week of Revival in Harrogate. Most of us plan to go."

"What about our lessons?"

"Assignments will be

GUESS	1. required."
	2. increased."
	3. excused."

"Since assignments are excused, I'll go too," Amy declared.

On the appointed evening, Amy and her friends slipped into back seats of the Methodist church. To Amy's surprise the revival meeting

GUESS	1. interested her.
	2. scared her.
	3. touched her.

The meeting touched Amy. She strained to hear the preacher's words. *It's nothing I haven't heard before,* she thought. *The difference is that this time I believe God*

GUESS	1. *calls me.*
	2. *wants me.*
	3. *loves me.*

The preacher quoted the Bible, "For God so loved the world that He gave His only begotten Son, that whosoever believeth in Him should not perish, but have everlasting life."*

* John 3:16.

19

As many times as I've heard that, I've never really believed it before, Amy realized. *Oh, Jesus, thank You for loving me. Take me into Your heart and come into mine.*

Amy

GUESS

1. believed.
2. rejected.
3. didn't care.

When Amy believed Christ died for her, she became a Christian. She sat silently on the back bench with her head bowed. The preacher prayed aloud, but Amy felt like she was in a great white place of glory with God reaching out to receive her as she ran into His arms.

Remembering this helped her in the troubled days ahead.

2

Belfast

The ship pulled into Belfast harbor, and tears flowed down Amy's cheeks. The tears showed her

GUESS	1. pain.
	2. sadness.
	3. joy.

Joy filled Amy's heart at the sight of her homeland. "I shouldn't cry," she rebuked herself, "but three years is a long time to be away." As the ship drew close to the busy, dirty shoreline, Amy could see

GUESS	1. Belfast Castle.
	2. Queens University.
	3. Mother and Father.

At the moment Amy was not interested in the Castle or University. She wanted to see her family. She peered at the large crowd on the wharf. "Oh, they are here. I know it!" Quickly she brushed the tears from her cheeks. "A big girl of fourteen doesn't cry, no matter how happy she is," Amy reminded herself.

Slowly she picked out people in the crowd. "There's Mother," she cried. A moment later, "And Father." One by one she counted the brothers and sisters,

GUESS	1. two, three, four.
	2. four, five, six.
	3. one, two, three.

Amy counted six, the two older boys, the two middle girls, and the two baby boys. The babies shocked Amy most, for they were now small boys wearing white sailor suits. *Will they even know me?* she wondered.

The ship docked, and now Amy could see her family waving frantically. "They see me!" she screamed and waved. No one heard her, however, as everyone else was screaming, waving, and yelling too.

The passengers waited impatiently while the gangplank was set in place. Then the scramble began. Amy ran down the plank

GUESS	1. first.
	2. last.
	3. squeezed in the middle.

Amy raced off first. She happened to be standing on the exact spot where the gangplank was attached.

Father caught her. Then Mother and one by one the prancing children claimed a hug. "Sure and it's good to see you again!" everyone exclaimed.

Amy collected her baggage, and the whole family trooped to the hired hack. "Where's our own carriage and horses?" Amy asked.

Father looked serious. "They were

| GUESS | 1. stolen." |
| | 2. sold." |

3. burned."

Father explained, "I had to sell all the animals. I'm afraid we haven't much money these days."

Amy bubbled, "I don't care, Father. We are all together now and going home. That's what matters. And everybody has grown so much! I'll have to get used to my *big* family."

Ethel, sitting on a stool, hugged Amy's leg. "And we can hardly believe our grown-up sister—such a difference between eleven and fourteen."

When they pulled up before the house, Amy tried to hide her surprise. Compared to their old home, this brick building was

GUESS	1. small.
	2. tall.
	3. big.

Though four stories tall, the house was squeezed between two other houses. Amy saw no tree-lined driveway or garden. Inside was better, though. She recognized the furniture, the rugs, and the pictures on the walls. "Mum, you brought our home with you to Belfast." She hugged her mother again. "It looks so good!"

She noticed

GUESS	1. the relief on Father's face.
	2. the squalling of the children.
	3. Father's sickly appearance.

Amy noticed Father looked relieved when she accepted everything. "Welcome to College Gardens!" he said.

Amy unpacked gifts for her family, and they ate dinner.

Then Davy suggested, "Let us boys take you exploring the neighborhood." The older boys helped Amy into a light coat and pulled her out the front door.

Ernest began the walk toward a huge estate. "This district is called College Gardens because the College sold its garden land to help pay for the new University about ten years ago." Amy acted

23

impressed with the three square towers.

"That's an old Tudor-style building," Davy explained, glad to display his newfound knowledge. "You'll be taking classes there, Father says."

"I will? Do you suppose Father will let me take what I want? Or do I have to learn what *they* say?"

"What do you want to study?" Davy asked.

Amy said she wanted to study

GUESS	1. music.
	2. painting.
	3. math.

"I choose music, singing, and painting." She laughed. "I've had enough math to last a lifetime."

Amy started to walk downhill.

"Not that way," Davy directed. "That's Shanty Town. We go there only on Sunday to take soup to the shut-ins. Mother insists, you know."

"Yes, we always gave soup to the poor. I'm glad that hasn't changed."

The boys pulled her toward Rosemary Avenue. "This is where the smart toffs live," Davy explained.

Amy admired the wide green lawns, the thick foliage, and the flowers. Most impressive were the mansions of the rich. At the end of the street stood the beautiful Rosemary Avenue Presbyterian Church.

"It's lovely," Amy gasped, pointing to the church.

"And we belong to it," Davy boasted.

Amy lifted her eyebrow, and Davy continued.

GUESS	1. "All our cousins belong."
	2. "The Carmichaels are leaders."
	3. "Our crowd is important."

"Counting all the cousins, the Carmichaels number sixteen."

"Now that I'm a Christian, I'd like to join, too."

"What do you mean a Christian? Weren't you always a Christian?"

Amy said,

<table>
<tr><td>GUESS</td><td>1. "For sure."
2. "A church member, yes."
3. "A Christian, no."</td></tr>
</table>

Amy said, "I often heard that Christ died for my sins, but now I believe. I *know* Jesus did it for me. To take *my* punishment."

Ernest changed the subject. "I wish I had time to show you Belfast Castle. It has a round tower and pointed roof. We can't walk around that roof like we did around our roof by the sea. Remember, Amy?"

"Do I!" Amy laughed, and they talked of childish pranks all the way home.

Amy looked around her new room on the fourth floor. She thought, *How nice to have a place alone after rooming with ten girls, but I wonder*

<table>
<tr><td>GUESS</td><td>1. *what the boys think.*
2. *if I will like the University.*
3. *if I belong here in Belfast.*</td></tr>
</table>

Amy wondered how she would fit into a new city.

She said her prayers and turned out the gaslight. Then she patted a space beside her on the bed. "Come sit and talk with me, Jesus. Tell me how I can live for You in Belfast."

"Come on, church is over," the brothers said as they rushed with Mother and Amy down windy Rosemary Avenue.

Mother said, "If you hurry you can take hot soup to the shutins and still get home in time for a late dinner."

But four blocks from the church they met a

1. family of kittens.

25

| GUESS | 2. ragged old woman. |
| | 3. mother duck with babies. |

Mrs. Carmichael approached the woman. "Do you need help, my dear? You look ill."

"Sure and you're so kind," the woman said. "I'm trying to get to me home." She pointed past the church.

Mother said, "Amy,

GUESS	1. walk on the other side."
	2. help the woman."
	3. ignore her."

Amy took the woman by one arm, while Ernest held her by the other. Together they almost lifted her light body off the ground. Her rags fluttered in the wind like feathers. They were now headed toward the church, and here came the church people on their way home.

The church members

GUESS	1. smiled in sympathy.
	2. lifted their noses.
	3. made remarks.

Though most well-dressed members pretended not to see the dreary sight, some made remarks such as,

GUESS	1. "What are those Carmichaels doing?"
	2. "The woman is tiddly for sure."
	3. "Can we help?"

Amy hated to be accused of being with a drunk woman. Her cheeks turned red. Then through the gray drizzle she remembered the Scripture about gold, silver, precious stones.

If any man's work abide, Amy remembered. Suddenly she

26

understood. *Nothing matters but the things eternal,* she thought.

Boldly she lifted her head and stared back into the eyes of the church people. *I'm not ashamed of helping one of God's creatures! Oh, Lord, I want to serve You. It doesn't matter what people say. Only eternal things count.*

Sour stares told her that not everyone agreed.

3

The Morning Watch

Amy threw open her windows one morning and exclaimed, "Oh, what a powerful day." She flung her arms wide and looked heavenward. "Thank You, Jesus, for bringing me home."
Amy was

```
┌─────────────┐
│             │   1. happy.
│   GUESS     │   2. sad.
│             │   3. disgusted.
└─────────────┘
```

Joy filled Amy's soul. She looked out the window at Belfast below, the dirty dock area, the business district, Shanty Town, and the mission district. Beneath the window, she saw

```
┌─────────────┐
│             │   1. College Gardens.
│   GUESS     │   2. Rosemary Avenue.
│             │   3. Oil Hill.
└─────────────┘
```

Just under her window she could see the rows of tall houses making up College Gardens.

"Oh, Jesus, I wish the people in those houses knew You love them!" Amy's prayers were

GUESS 1. just talking.
2. solemn.
3. personal.

Amy just talked to Jesus when she prayed.

At breakfast next morning Amy said, "We always had a Bible talk around the breakfast table at Harrogate."

"But we don't have time here," Father said. Then he left for Uncle William's new mill.

The children began scattering for the day. When Amy didn't move, Ethel sat back down, and Ava turned in the doorway. "What you going to do?" she asked.

"Pray with Amy," Ethel answered coolly. Amy was

GUESS 1. surprised.
2. interested.
3. ready.

Amy said, "I'm surprised you suggested it, but come to my room. We can look out the window. There we can see and pray for the whole city." Amy held out her hands to her little sisters, and together they climbed the stairs.

"Let's sing some choruses first," she suggested. The three sang so loudly that little James and Phillip soon peeked around the door to see what was happening. Amy invited them to come in, and she told them all a Bible story. Amy didn't know it, but Davy and Ernest were sitting on the steps outside.

"Let's do this every morning," Ethel suggested, when Amy said the lesson was over.

"Can we, Amy? Can we?" the children clamored.

Amy answered,

1. "Yes."

2. "No."
3. "Maybe."

Amy smiled into the eyes of her sisters and brothers. "We can call it the Morning Watch," she said.

Davy and Ernest soon joined the others. For some time only the Carmichael children met together. But when a new family moved next door, Davy said,

1. "Let's skip the meetings."
2. "Let the boys come."
3. "Let's turn cartwheels."

Davy and Ernest begged Amy to invite the neighbor boys. "Let's ask Mother," Amy suggested.

Mrs. Carmichael admitted, "I listened at the stairway myself." She smiled. "Why not have a meeting Saturday morning for all the neighborhood children? We can fold up the table and use the dining room. I'll even serve cookies and tea afterward."

Amy hugged her mother.

When Saturday came,

1. no one came to the meeting.
2. only the Carmichaels attended.
3. several neighbors came.

Many neighborhood children tumbled into the house, and Amy acted out a Bible story. Every week the dining room rang with joyful singing. By taking out the chairs they made room for all on the rug.

Later the preacher at the Rosemary Church heard of the Morning Watch and asked the children why they went. They answered,

1. "We pray."
2. "We love Amy."
3. "There are no dull moments."

30

The children told Pastor Parks, "There are no dull moments in Amy's class."

After that Dr. Parks invited Amy to hold her meetings in

| GUESS |

1. the garden.
2. the church hall.
3. the pastor's home.

"Come," Dr. Parks invited, "hold your meetings in the church hall on Sunday mornings. There is plenty of room there."

Amy was pleased. "Then the children could sit on chairs instead of on the floor. Thank you, Dr. Parks."

But the children objected. "We don't want to give up the Morning Watch."

Amy finally convinced them to

| GUESS |

1. come on Sunday.
2. meet both Saturday and Sunday.
3. meet on Saturday.

"Sure and we'll have two meetings," she said. "And since there is plenty of room in the church hall, I'll invite the

| GUESS |

1. mill workers."
2. Shawlies."
3. old women."

"I'll invite the Shawlies and their brothers of Shanty Town to the class, that I will," Amy decided.

"But will they come to the Rosemary Street Church?" Mother questioned. "Will they feel welcome in that fine building? Will the members welcome them?"

"Of course they'll be welcomed," Amy said. "Isn't the church the house of God? And didn't Jesus say, 'Let the little children come unto Me?' "

Mother answered,

31

GUESS	1. "Jesus will welcome them." 2. "The church members will welcome them." 3. "The pastor will welcome them."

"That is right," Mother said. "Jesus will welcome them. That's all that matters."

The Shawlies slid into the pews with their ragged dresses and dirty shawls over their heads. Amy saw their faces brighten as she explained the Bible to them. Songs rang through the church. Amy's class grew until, a year later, they filled the church hall.

But not everyone was happy. Some church members said,

GUESS	1. "Why are these filthy children here?" 2. "Why don't they stay in Shanty Town?" 3. "Jesus can't love them!"

No one said Jesus didn't love the children, and no one said Amy didn't love them. Many church members, however, complained, "Why don't they stay in Shanty Town where they belong?"

The church leaders met and told the pastor, "Tell Amy to

GUESS	1. stop the meetings." 2. enlarge the meetings." 3. move the meetings."

The leaders demanded that she move the meetings.

"But where can we go?" Amy asked when the preacher told her this news.

"You will need a building," he answered.

At home Mother comforted her. "I know you are only nineteen and could never build a hall, but, honey, you know Someone who can."

"I do?" Amy asked, dropping into a chair. "Who?"

Mother replied,

1. "Father."

"Why don't they stay in Shanty Town?"

GUESS	2. "Mr. Richard." 3. "God."

"God owns the cattle on a thousand hills. He can provide a building if you believe Him. You know the Shawlies will pray with you."

Everyone prayed, "Please, God, give us a place."

Soon Amy received a letter from a lady named Miss Kate Mitchell. It said, "Come see me. I hear you need a building in which to hold children's meetings."

Amy visited Miss Mitchell's beautiful home. Miss Kate told her,

GUESS	1. "A building costs too much." 2. "You are too young to manage it." 3. "I'll pay for the building."

Miss Mitchell said, "I'll buy a metal building for you. I'll do more than that—I'll move to Belfast to help you manage everything."

When the builders finished, Amy and Miss Kate stood in the street, admiring the building.

"What will you call this place?" Miss Kate inquired. Amy answered,

GUESS	1. "The Jesus Place." 2. "The Shanty Church." 3. "The Welcome."

Amy said, "I'll call it 'The Welcome.' "

Miss Kate hugged Amy. "It looks like a loaf pan turned upside down. But what does it matter if everyone is welcome?"

34

4

The Welcome

"**O**h, Amy, I'm so happy about the building," Father rejoiced. "You see, I've always told you never to give in to difficulty."

Amy gave her father a hug and was shocked because

GUESS

1. his body felt so thin.
2. she could feel his ribs.
3. he felt so solid and strong.

When Amy felt her father's ribs through his coat, she knew something was wrong. She wanted to ask questions, but everyone was so happy about The Welcome that she said nothing just then.

The day before the dedication of The Welcome, Amy hurried along a street in Shanty Town. She wanted to finish painting the banner that was to hang over the platform. In front of her, she saw

GUESS

1. a crying child.
2. a wounded bird.
3. a roaring lion.

"Why are you crying?" Amy asked the little girl.

"Oh, it's you, Miss Amy!" The child flew into her arms and cried.

"Let's sit down on this rock," Amy said. "Here, let me hold you on my lap."

By patting the child's hair and coaxing her with kind words, Amy persuaded the girl to tell her of

> GUESS

1. beatings.
2. abuse.
3. picnics.

"Why didn't you run away when the man touched you?" Amy asked.

"There is no place to go." The tear-stained face turned upward to Amy.

"Yes, there is. See that new metal building in the next block? The sign says, 'The Welcome.' There is no lock on the door, and anyone is welcome to come in to escape danger."

The next day Amy spoke at the dedication. "The name means what it says. All are welcome. Yes, meetings and classes are planned, but any time you are in danger, you can find a place of safety at The Welcome." Many children in the crowd

> GUESS

1. laughed.
2. did not understand.
3. were grateful.

Though some did not understand, others were grateful for a place to find help and safety. Amy didn't know how God would use her to protect abused children in the future.

With Miss Kate's help Amy was soon holding classes about being safe and clean. The little girls

> GUESS

1. washed their hair.
2. killed lice.

36

3. laundered clothes.

"The Welcome is a place for learning—learning physical skills like washing, as well as for learning spiritual truths," Amy said.

"Let's have some Bible meetings," Miss Kate suggested. "And I know who the speaker should be—

```
┌──────────┐   1. Amy."
│  GUESS   │   2. Dr. Parks."
└──────────┘   3. two students."
```

Miss Kate had heard of two students from the Moody Bible Institute in Chicago, who were in Belfast. "Let's invite them to hold the first meetings in The Welcome."

Amy agreed and painted a large banner for the platform. It said, "That in all things, He may have the preeminence." Amy looked into the sea of faces from Shanty Town. *How I love these children,* she thought.

At the revival meeting

```
┌──────────┐   1. they sang a new hymn.
│  GUESS   │   2. people believed in Jesus.
└──────────┘   3. Amy disappeared.
```

People came to know Christ.

After the meetings the children of Shanty Town came to The Welcome any time they liked. One day at lunch time, they said, "We are hungry." Since Amy had nothing to give them, she said,

```
┌──────────┐   1. "Go home and eat."
│  GUESS   │   2. "I have no food."
└──────────┘   3. "Let's pray."
```

Amy looked into their hungry faces and said, "Let's pray." While the children were praying, a well-dressed gentleman slipped inside the doorway. He stayed a minute, listening to the children. Then he left some money on a table near the door and disappeared. The money was enough for

1. lunch for a few.
2. lunch for Amy.
3. lunch for all.

All exclaimed, "What a good lunch!"

In time The Welcome developed many activities besides Bible classes. Amy often took the little children outside to play circle games, while their older sisters sewed with Miss Kate.

Even Mother taught a class called Home Evening. It was for the parents.

Another hard problem really troubled Amy. Finally she told Miss Kate, "I cannot come to The Welcome for a while. Father grows weaker every day. He took a chill and now has to stay in bed."

Amy stayed at Father's side, reading, telling stories, and praying. After Christmas, he became worse, and at last Mr. Carmichael

1. recovered.
2. died.
3. was paralyzed.

On April 12, 1885, Father asked that Amy sing "My Faith Looks Up to Thee, Thou Lamb of Calvary, Saviour Divine." As Amy sang, the church bells rang for Sunday service, and Mr. Carmichael died.

Amy

1. felt crushed.
2. rejoiced in the Lord.
3. felt angry.

"Maybe I should be glad he's with Jesus," Amy sobbed, as

Miss Kate hugged her. "But I'm not. There's an empty space in my heart, and I know it's for him."

After the funeral she felt better. "Now that I can accept God's will," Amy promised her mother, "I'll help you

GUESS

1. earn money for the family."
2. care for the smaller children."
3. keep the garden."

Amy said, "I will help you care for the smaller children."

For several years Amy worked in The Welcome and also cared for the children at home. But the day finally came when the family was forced to break up.

Ernest and Davy went

GUESS

1. to England.
2. to France.
3. to America.

The older boys went to America. "We can start a new life in a new land," Davy assured her. Later James moved to Canada with a neighboring family. And little Phillip became a cabin boy on a ship and went to South Africa.

Then Mother herself accepted a job

GUESS

1. selling lace.
2. managing a mission.
3. sweeping chimneys.

Mother became a manager for a city mission and moved to another city. Ethel and Ava went there with her.

"I'm dizzy with these changes," Amy wailed to Miss Kate. "What can it mean?"

"You are now free to work full time for the Lord," Miss Kate assured her. "Don't worry about The Welcome, my dear. I'll always be here."

"Too many changes, too fast," Amy said. Then she became very ill. She turned to her old friend. "The whole family is gone. Oh, Miss Kate, what shall I do? Where shall I go?"

Miss Kate contacted a friend, Mr. Robert Wilson, and the Wilson family invited Amy to come to Broughton Grange until she was well.

She said,

GUESS

1. "Yes, thank you."
2. "I don't want to bother you."
3. "I guess so."

Amy hesitated. *How can I accept help from strangers?* she wondered. Once she moved to Broughton Grange, however, her health began to improve. She felt more cheerful, too, as she

GUESS

1. studied the Bible.
2. rode in the one-horse buggy.
3. wrote stories.

She called Mr. Wilson the Dear Old Man (D.O.M. for short) and rode with him in a one-horse buggy. Together they plotted stories about Amy's experiences with the Shawlies. One day Amy received a magazine called *Bright Words*. Amy and the D.O.M.'s family jumped up and down when they saw one of Amy's stories printed in the magazine.

Amy used her time at Broughton Grange as a time for

GUESS

1. learning lessons.
2. training animals.
3. growing flowers.

Amy and the old man sat and talked on the veranda. "I'm learning lessons I may need," she said, "but I don't know why."

On Wednesday evening, January 13, 1892, Amy found out why. That evening she went to her room, knelt beside her bed, and asked the Lord, "What do You wish me to do?"

In her heart she seemed to hear the answer, "Go ye."

It is God speaking to me, she thought.

She wrote to her mother saying,

GUESS

1. "God says, 'Go.' "
2. "I will stay."
3. "I must be mistaken."

Amy wrote, "He says, 'Go.' I cannot stay."

"How can I go to a foreign land and leave my mother and sisters?" She worried while waiting for her mother's answer. "There are thousands who have never heard the gospel, but I don't know where God wants me." So many questions filled her head that she was dizzy.

When she got a letter from her mother, it said,

GUESS

1. "You belong to God."
2. "Go where the Lord pleases."
3. "Stay home with me."

Mother said, "Dearest Amy, God has lent you to me all these years. You were a strength, comfort, and joy to me, but you are God's. Go where He leads you. I give you back into His loving arms. I say, 'Take her, dear Lord. Use her in Thy service and for Thy glory.' "

Amy lay the letter on her bed and kneeled down beside it. "Thank You, Lord!"

With Mother's blessing, Amy had enough courage to tell the D.O.M. that God had called her to be a missionary.

Mr. Wilson agreed, and together they went to the Keswick Convention. There Amy met Hudson Taylor, who had started the China Inland Mission. She said, "I offer myself for service, not knowing the place where God wants me."

The Keswick Mission Committee prayed, and thought, and decided

41

GUESS

1. to put up a new building.
2. to send Amy as a missionary.
3. that Amy should stay at home.

When the Committee voted to send Amy overseas as a missionary, she said, "This is the proof of God's call."

5

Foreign Soil

Not everyone was happy about Amy's plans to be a missionary. While she packed her clothes, members of the D.O.M.'s family said,

GUESS

1. "You musn't leave your mother."
2. "Your sisters need you."
3. "The Dear Old Man will be lonely."

"Don't you know you are leaving the Dear Old Man to a lonely life? Think how much he has done for you. When you came, you were sick; now you look strong and healthy. You should be ashamed."

But Amy knew she

GUESS

1. must obey God.
2. couldn't please everyone.
3. was only one person.

Amy was torn between going and staying. "I know I can't

please everyone," she said. "The D.O.M. wants me to follow the Lord's leading, and I will."

She took the train to London. Timidly she knocked at the door of the China Inland Mission. "Come in, come in," a young woman invited. Several other new missionaries also welcomed her.

When she saw Hudson Taylor again, he encouraged her. "God will show you

| GUESS |

1. where He wants you to go."
2. the way home."
3. if you are qualified."

Though the missionary training stressed the need in China, Hudson Taylor did not push Amy. "God will show you where He wants you to go, my dear. Just be patient," he advised.

Amy listened closely as Hudson Taylor himself gave daily Bible talks. She had always had trouble

| GUESS |

1. keeping her temper.
2. obeying rules.
3. helping others.

Amy said, "I hate following rules."
One rule Hudson Taylor stressed was

| GUESS |

1. Be on time.
2. Always carry a Bible.
3. Dress like the natives.

When Hudson Taylor was in China, he dressed like the Chinese. He asked all his missionaries to do this. But Amy saw no reason to do so. "I know I would look awful and feel awful," she grumbled to another missionary. "It seems I should be able to wear the clothes I like."

"Well, just don't tell Mr. Taylor," the woman advised her.

44

When missionary training school was over, they celebrated their graduation with a gala dinner. The room was filled with hopeful new missionaries eager to sail to China.

After some speeches, Hudson Taylor stood up and said, "Here is a letter from Japan. Mr. and Mrs. F. Burton are asking for help. They need

| GUESS | 1. six missionaries."
| | 2. one missionary."
| | 3. money."

Amy listened to Mr. Taylor read the last sentence of the letter: "Is someone there willing to take this leap into Japan with us?"

Amy stood up. "I will go," she said.

With the other new missionaries Amy sailed as far as Shanghai, China. Then by herself she took a steamer to Japan. "I have to pinch myself to believe I am really here," she said.

Amy believed she was in Japan, however, on April 25, 1893, when a little tugboat met the steamer and put her off in the rain with her trunk and bags. Sitting on her trunk there on the wharf she looked at her ship, which would soon sail away. She looked around at the jabbering Japanese and the strange shoreline. She could not see

| GUESS | 1. a familiar face.
| | 2. a welcoming smile.
| | 3. a white cat.

Obviously no one had come to meet her. *But how could they meet me?* Amy asked herself. *No one knows when the ship arrived.* She stared in dismay at the coolies, who fought with each other to carry her bags. They screamed at each other in Japanese. As the rain poured over her and her luggage, she muttered, "My hat, oh, my hat is ruined." Suddenly she felt silly worrying about a hat. She laughed out loud.

A young man stepped up to her and said,

45

GUESS

1. "I'm French."
2. "I'm English."
3. "I'm American."

"I'm American," the young man said and scolded her. "How can you laugh here in the rain? Don't you know of the dreadful things that could happen to you? Where do you want to go anyway?"

Amy handed the young man an envelope with an address on it. Quickly he gave the dock helpers orders in Japanese, helped load her things in two rickshaws, and escorted her to the Burton's house. Once the Burtons welcomed her, he disappeared.

"Oh, I wanted to thank him!" Amy turned on the steps of the small porch. She looked past the tiny lawn and the iron lamp posts, but the street was empty. She looked around at her trunk and bags and said,

GUESS

1. "What a fine looking American."
2. "I gave him a tract."
3. "God must have sent him."

"I'm glad that I gave him a leaflet explaining how to go to heaven."

Amy's missionary life in Japan began right away. No one waited to learn the language before beginning Christian work in Japan, because

GUESS

1. all the Japanese understood English.
2. they used a translator, Misaki San.
3. God put Japanese words in their mouths.

"Thank God for Misaki San!" Amy rejoiced. "I can understand nothing of this jibberish."

Together with the interpreter, she began visiting Japanese homes. One day an old woman slid open her bamboo door.

Misaki San bowed low and explained, "Amy is a missionary.

She came to give you a message from God."

The woman invited them in and served tea, as they sat on the floor. She listened as Misaki San repeated Amy's words in Japanese. The woman seemed interested in knowing the way to heaven. But suddenly

GUESS

1. Amy fainted.
2. the woman noticed Amy's fur gloves.
3. Misaki San became ill.

The woman felt Amy's fur gloves and the material of her dress.
"Don't think of my clothes!" Amy exclaimed. "Think of Christ!" But they could not get the woman to think of Christ again. Finally Amy gave the woman her gloves and left in despair. They walked slowly home, and Amy

GUESS

1. bought new gloves.
2. scolded Misaki San.
3. changed into Japanese clothes.

Amy put on a Japanese kimono and said, "I'll never again risk losing a soul for so little a thing as gloves. Hudson Taylor was right. I see why he made that clothing rule for his Chinese missionaries. Why, oh why, is my head so stubborn?"

On the morning of her twenty-sixth birthday, Amy asked Misaki San, "I wonder what will happen on this birthday?" What happened was that four Japanese came to believe in the Lord. "Best present I ever had," she said. "Now let us pray for those eight Buddhists that we will visit tomorrow."

The next day she and Misaki San set out on foot to a nearby village named Hirose. At their meeting, seven out of the eight people wanted to trust Jesus. It was now very late, but Amy kept talking with the eighth man, a fifty-year-old grandfather.

"Come." Misaki San tugged at her sleeve. "He's been a slave to drugs all his life. Forget about him."

But Amy continued to talk about his need to be free from drugs. "Only God can make you free," she told him.

47

Finally he prayed,

```
┌─────────┐   1. "Send these people away."
│  GUESS  │   2. "Honorable God, please forgive."
└─────────┘   3. "Please to wash."
```

Amy and Misaki San rejoiced as they heard the old man's prayer, "Please to forgive, please to wash."

Later as they hurried along the deserted streets, Amy prayed, "Thank You, Jesus, for forgiving and washing the man's soul clean."

Not everyone accepted the words of the Bible, however. In another small city, Buddhist priests stopped Amy on the street and demanded,

```
┌─────────┐   1. "Are you a foreign devil?"
│  GUESS  │   2. "We want to see the Bible lived."
└─────────┘   3. "Can you show Jesus to us?"
```

The priests spoke kindly. "We have heard much preaching. Can you show us the life of your Lord Jesus? We want to see it lived!"

Amy thought about that. She prayed that she would have the spirit of Jesus and show it every day. After a while she had earned a new name. The Japanese called her

```
┌─────────┐   1. a foreign devil.
│  GUESS  │   2. the Jesus-walking woman.
└─────────┘   3. the selfish one.
```

The Japanese called her the Jesus-walking woman.

After Amy had been in Japan about a year, she

```
┌─────────┐   1. cried.
│  GUESS  │   2. became ill.
└─────────┘
```

48

3. was tired of the place.

Amy became seriously ill with the "Japanese head," as the doctor called her sickness. She knew she should leave Japan in order to get well. "But what will people say if I come home too soon?" she worried. So she stayed.

While resting, Amy wrote a book about Japan called *From Sunrise Land.* But she refused to go home until one day she got a letter saying,

GUESS

1. "Your mother is dying."
2. "The D.O.M. has had a stroke."
3. "Your sister needs you."

Amy left on the first ship to England. "The Dear Old Man has had a stroke, and he needs me," she wrote to her mother. During the entire trip she herself was so sick that she could not leave her cabin.

6

Madcap

"I could be happy this Christmas, if only I were not

GUESS

1. so lonely."
2. so sick."
3. so full of hate."

Amy was still sick when she reached England in 1894. She took a train to Manchester. As it chugged into the station she could see her mother and sisters on the platform to meet her. "Just the sight of them makes me feel better," she murmured to herself.

Amy rushed into her mother's arms. She was surprised at the length of her mother's hug. "I'll be here awhile, Mother," she cried, wiggling herself free. "Let me hug Ethel and Ava, too." After all the greetings, everybody rode home in a hired hack, laughing and talking so fast that Amy could hardly hear all the news.

As soon as she heard that the Dear Old Man was better, Amy relaxed in the love of her family.

"You are to go to Broughton Grange to see him in a few weeks," Ethel said. "But for now, you are ours."

Once inside her mother's home, Amy said, "Oh, I'm so tired." She sank exhausted onto a couch.

"Tell us everything that happened. Tell us!" Ava demanded. Amy held her sister close and patted her golden hair. "Promise never to go away again!" Ava demanded.

Amy promised

	1. to stay always.
GUESS	2. to follow God's leading.
	3. to be a mother to Ava.

Amy couldn't promise anything more than to follow God's leading. "I know, I know how you feel, Ava. I wish I could promise, but once I'm strong again, I'll wait for God's call."

"This is only a detour," Mother said. "But let's all enjoy the scenery on the detour." Mother and Ethel understood, but Ava pleaded, "Please stay, please, please stay."

All too soon the weeks flew by, and Amy went

	1. back to Japan.
GUESS	2. to China.
	3. to Broughton Grange.

Still very weak, Amy managed to get to Broughton Grange by train. "The D.O.M. couldn't meet you," his family explained as they brought her to the house to see him.

The D.O.M. was happy to see Amy again. "It seems to take illness to bring us together," he said. "Sickness is a test. Do you use your religion then, or do you lose your religion?"

Amy smiled. "We'll never lose it!"

As the days passed, they both felt better. The Dear Old Man answered a million questions, always from the Bible. "You can't worry and trust at the same time," the D.O.M. reminded her.

One day as they sat on the veranda overlooking the sunny garden, the D.O.M. said, "I hear that

| | 1. your book is selling well." |
| GUESS | 2. your book is causing concern for Japan." |

51

3. your book is causing people to pray."

Amy was pleased. "I'm glad people's eyes are opened to the needs of Japan, and that they pray. But I'm getting restless again. As God gives me strength and the pains in my head go away, I want to serve Him again."

"No need to think of a tropical land. The doctor would never allow it, you know."

"I know." Amy stood up and paced restlessly. "But they say, when one door closes, another opens."

When she saw the mailman coming, she

GUESS

1. shouted to the D.O.M.
2. ran to the mailbox.
3. raced around the garden.

Reaching into the mailbox, she pulled out a letter with a strange stamp. It was from Bangalore, a city in

GUESS

1. Alaska.
2. Japan.
3. India.

The letter was from India, and Amy rushed to the veranda to share it. "It's from the lady in charge of the Church of England hospital in Bangalore, South India."

"Read it! Hurry!" the D.O.M. demanded as soon as Amy had settled into a chair.

"She says the climate is healthy, delightful in fact. And, oh, she asks if I will

GUESS

1. pray for her."
2. come and help her."
3. send money."

"She wants you to come to India?" Mr. Wilson controlled his voice. "I'm surprised the Church of England Missionary Society would make such a request. Are you sure they want a Presbyterian?"

Amy said,

GUESS

1. "It's not the church that matters."
2. "It's devotion to Christ that counts."
3. "It's generous of the Church of England."

Amy declared, "You know it's devotion to Christ that counts in the life of a missionary. Do you suppose the Keswick Committee would still pay my salary if I went to India?"

By July 1895, the doctors had examined Amy and passed her for India. The Committee then

GUESS

1. talked with Amy.
2. accepted Amy.
3. rejected Amy.

"Amy, you are accepted as a missionary to India," they said.

Amy hugged everyone on the committee. "You are real friends to stick by me. I won't come home in a year this time! I promise."

"Don't worry, my dear," Mr. Wilson said. "The average person doesn't succeed at first."

Amy spent several days saying good-bye to her mother and sisters. Together they celebrated the D.O.M.'s seventieth birthday. Amy said, "Forget your birthdays, and keep your enthusiasm." But she could not hide her hot tears. She knew

GUESS

1. she might never see them again.
2. she'd be back in a year.
3. India was a dangerous place.

Since the Mission Society had no plan for furloughs, she knew she might never see any of them again. Amy called these good-byes "blistering" days. Still, in spite of an aching heart, she boarded a steamer and reached India on November 9, 1895.

It was spring in India. Flowers bloomed everywhere. The sun shone warmly, and

GUESS	1. five missionaries met her.
	2. one missionary came.
	3. ten missionaries greeted her.

Five missionaries hugged her in welcome. Once the baggage was settled, they all boarded a carriage belonging to the mission. The ride to Bangalore was delightful. Amy could hardly answer questions, she was so busy looking at the tall trees and green fields. "It seems so strange," she bubbled. "I just finished summer in England, and here it is spring again."

When they reached the mission property, she was impressed with

GUESS	1. the large hospital.
	2. the school buildings.
	3. the pleasant missionary quarters.

"After Japan, where the missionaries live simply, I didn't expect such beauty and comfort!" Amy exclaimed. Servants scampered to meet every need. One young woman made Amy's bed, and another cleaned her room. Even the food was elaborate.

During her first week, she had several more surprises.

GUESS	1. The teachers were Muslims.
	2. The doctors were Hindu.
	3. The missionaries were managers.

"Why are none of these teachers and doctors Christians?" Amy asked at the dinner table. "Muslims and Hindus won't spread the Christian gospel."

"There *are no* Christian teachers or doctors," Miss Carr, the lady in charge, explained.

"What! No converts?"

"Not in the fifteen years I've been here." Miss Carr shook her head.

"But surely the interpreters can explain the way of salvation."

"There are no interpreters."

"Why not?" Amy protested. "We had plenty in Japan."

"Neither Hindus nor Muslims would repeat your words truly. Never would they speak contrary to their own religion."

"Then I'll

GUESS	1. learn the Urdu tongue." 2. learn the language of Zenana." 3. learn Tamil."

"I'll learn their language then," Amy declared. "Whether it be Urdu or Tamil. I want to win people to Christ. That's why I came."

Miss Carr looked thoughtfully at Amy.

"All right, Miss Madcap!" she exclaimed.

Amy was startled. "Madcap, you call me?"

"Yes, I saw you racing the horses up the hill yesterday. I'm afraid you

GUESS	1. haven't learned to be proper." 2. race around like a hare." 3. don't act like an English missionary."

Miss Carr accused Amy. "I see you do not act like a proper missionary."

And a week later she called Amy into her office.

"Amy, dear," she said. "The staff has been discussing the matter. We feel you would be happier in the evangelistic part of our mission. You are neither an Indian teacher, a doctor, or nurse, and as you say yourself, you came to win people to Christ."

"Oh, I did. That is what I loved so much in Japan," Amy agreed. "Only, of course, it is Jesus who does the saving, not me."

"We have a Mr. Walker and his wife, who live in Tinnevelly District under primitive conditions. They are experts in the Tamil language. They hold meetings with the Indians. Would you be willing to help them?"

Amy asked,

GUESS

1. "Would I have a nice room?"
2. "Would they teach me?"
3. "When can I go?"

Amy asked, "When can I start?"

"Not so fast. These things take time. I'll send a messenger to Tinnevelly tomorrow. In the meantime, you can begin studying the Tamil language with one of our teachers. He's not as good as Walker, but he can stay ahead of *you,* no doubt."

Amy rushed to her room and wrote a long letter to her mother. She prayed, "Thank You, Jesus, for this chance to do something. I feel so helpless here—and so useless with all these servants."

By Christmas, Amy was on her way to

GUESS

1. Ooty.
2. Tinnevelly District.
3. England.

Amy climbed into a farmer's cart. Then she squatted on her trunk and clutched the sides of the cart with sweaty hands. Miss Carr directed the farmer to take her to Mr. Walker in Ooty, Tinnevelly District. "Good-bye, Miss Carr," Amy said without tears. "Thank you for your kindness."

The cart had no springs, and every bump jolted her bones, but Amy was interested only in what the future held. "What will the Walkers be like? What kind of place is Ooty? Will the Indians be my friends?"

She looked at the farmer. *I'd ask you questions, but I know you couldn't understand a single word I say,* she thought. *The Christmas season is here, and it's hot—like the middle of summer in Ireland. How strange!*

Would she ever get used to India?

7

The Walkers

The Walkers welcomed a tired and sweaty Amy as though she

GUESS

1. was a lost friend.
2. intended to hurt them.
3. was a stranger.

Amy felt like a friend at once.

Jane, as Mrs. Walker insisted on being called, fairly flew about, getting Amy settled. "If you need anything, let us know."

Her husband asked Amy to call him Walker. " 'Mr.' is not necessary," he said. And he agreed to teach her the Tamil language.

As they sat drinking tea in the cheerful yellow kitchen, he asked,

GUESS

1. "Why did you come here?"
2. "How much do you want to know of Tamil?"
3. "Can we be friends?"

Walker asked, "How much Tamil do you want to know?"

"Why, I want to know enough to win souls, and a little over."

Amy stared back into his eyes for a long moment.

Walker realized she was serious, and he answered from his heart. "And you shall have 'a little over.' "

The Walkers' plain home was nothing compared to the elaborate houses the other missionaries had. Jane worried. "Amy, I hope you don't mind making your own bed and cleaning your room. We decided we did not want to make servants of the Indian people."

"Me, either," Amy declared. "I'd rather treat them as equals. I know Jesus loves them as much as He loves us."

Walker said,

GUESS

1. "We will never be able to work together."
2. "We will work well together."
3. "I doubt if our ideas agree."

The older missionary smiled. "We'll work well together, I see."

In the days that followed, Amy felt like she had an older brother. Walker

GUESS

1. teased her.
2. scolded her.
3. whipped her.

"You are too impatient," Walker teased Amy. "The language comes to you when you do not try so hard."

Amy told Jane later, "Walker is a true friend. He calms my soul."

The missionaries decided they would speak only Tamil. This forced Amy to learn more words. Another thing that helped her understand was

GUESS

1. jumping rope.
2. singing in Tamil.
3. painting the landscape.

Amy led the singing.

Amy could soon sing in Tamil. Walker had translated several songs like "Jesus Loves Me" and "Jesus Wants Me for a Sunbeam" into Tamil. Since she knew the English, she could understand the Tamil words of the song. Walker, Jane, and Amy held meetings in nearby villages. The children watched with large brown eyes as Amy led the singing with her sweet voice. Amy could do this because of her

GUESS	1. pretty face.
	2. lovely Indian dress.
	3. singing lessons in Belfast.

The music I learned in Belfast helps me now, she realized. She wore a sari like the women of Tinnevelly wore. Sometimes, however, she confused the Indian people, because she put on a man's straw hat to protect her skin from the sun.

One day she overheard some children discussing her.

"She isn't a man."

"Yes, he is."

"She isn't."

"He has a man's hat!"

"But look at her dress!"

Though Amy could not understand every word, she laughed at the argument. As her Tamil improved, she could finally answer questions like, "Are you married or a widow?" "What relatives do you have?" "Where are they?" "Why did you leave them to come here?"

One question they always asked was, "How much money do you get for talking to us?"

As they rode back to Ooty in the wagon, Amy asked Walker, "Why do they always ask about my salary?"

He answered,

GUESS	1. "They are curious."
	2. "They think you are greedy."
	3. "They can't understand working because of love."

60

"They judge you by themselves." Walked laughed. "No one works for love here. If I want someone to help me move a heavy box, I must pay. If I want a believer to tell others how he found Christ, he asks how much I pay."

"How much *do* you pay?" Suddenly Amy was alarmed. These ideas were new to her.

"I don't pay. I tell them to do it for love of Jesus or not at all."

Amy sighed in relief. "I agree. At The Welcome no one was paid. Even Miss Kate, who bought the building, was not paid."

"It's a different land, Amy, and a different people," Walker reminded her.

Amy studied long, long hours to learn the Tamil language. Years later, when people said, "You speak like a native Indian. It must be easy for you," Amy remembered

GUESS	1. the days of study.
	2. the nights of study.
	3. the years of study.

It took less than two years to learn enough Tamil to preach, but it took Amy forty years to learn "a little bit more."

When Amy could tell a Bible story and give an invitation to the village people, she enjoyed the meetings. But as she spoke, some always interrupted.

GUESS	1. "How much did that sari cost?"
	2. "What food do you eat?"
	3. "Do you eat curry and rice, as we do?"

No matter how serious Amy was about spiritual things, someone would ask, "What do you eat?" "Is that dress silk?"

Walker advised her, "Answer their questions first, then give the gospel message. At first the Indians are more interested in the vessel than in the contents."

When they went on gospel trips from city to city, Walker took six Christian men with him. "The men visit homes and invite the people to come to the town square, near the village well," Walker explained. "Then we hold meetings there with music, singing, and preaching."

Amy listened to the Indian Christians. She saw the interest on the faces of the people. She realized

GUESS

1. they believed their own people.
2. the foreigner is more important.
3. the music is best.

Amy realized the Indians believed their own people more easily than a foreigner.

Another thing that bothered Amy was what was called the caste system. Amy asked Walker about the system one morning at breakfast.

"Do you mean that if a man is the son of a wood-carver, he must

GUESS

1. be a wood-carver, too?"
2. marry the daughter of a wood-carver?"
3. pay taxes?"

Walker explained. "He must do *all those things*. He can never change unless, of course, he loses caste." He sipped his tea.

"What do you mean?" Amy asked, as she ate her eggs and rice. Jane broke in. "To lose caste means he

GUESS

1. becomes nobody."
2. belongs to the important class."
3. is an outcast."

"An outcast belongs to no one, is nothing. He cannot work at any job belonging to a caste."

"But how does he live?" Amy's brow wrinkled.

"Sometimes he starves. At best he does work no one else will do, like planting rice, where one stoops all day knee-deep in water," Walker said.

"What if he is a Christian?"

"I hate to tell you this—" Walker shook his head sadly "—but if a man of the highest caste became a Christian, he would be thrown out of the caste."

"Do you know of anyone who did this?"

Walker shook his head again and said,

GUESS	1. "Yes, many."
	2. "No, no one."
	3. "Never."

The missionary said, "I know of no one of the highest caste who is a Christian!"

"But we have large crowds at our meetings. They listen, and a few always receive Christ."

"Amy, you are too new here to know it, but those who come to Christ are of the lowest caste—or of no caste."

Jane spoke up. "Does that hurt you, Amy?"

"No, God loves them all no matter what their caste." Amy looked out the window at the blueness of the sky. She felt God gave her the answer. "We can only give the Word and be thankful for those who accept."

"Even," said Walker, "if that means you and I are rated as one

GUESS	1. of the highest caste."
	2. of no caste."
	3. of the lower caste."

Walker explained, "If you, as a foreigner, are friends with the high caste, you are treated as they are. If you are friends with the outcasts, you, too, are considered an outcast."

Amy grinned. "I personally don't care. I came here to tell the good news to whoever will listen. I've been called a *madcap*. Why should I worry if someone wants to call me an *outcast?*"

Jane came over to Amy and hugged her. "You are the prettiest little outcast I ever saw," she joked. "Who called you a madcap?"

"One of the high caste, I believe." Amy looked wise but would say no more.

8

The Starry Cluster

Walker called his band of men workers "my Indian brothers." One morning as Amy and Jane washed the breakfast dishes, Amy had an idea.

"Could I have a band of

GUESS	1. Indian men?"
	2. Indian sisters?"
	3. Indian children?"

"Would it be possible for me to have a band of Indian sisters?" Amy hesitated. "To travel about with me and hold meetings as Walker does with the men?"

Jane answered,

GUESS	1. "It is impossible."
	2. "It is unbecoming."
	3. "It has never been done."

Jane looked thoughtful. "You know, such a thing has never

been done in India. It would not be easy to find six women willing to do that, even for considerable money."

"Oh, but I would not pay them *anything.*" Amy frowned. "You know how the people won't believe what we say because they think we are paid to say it."

"In that case, you can forget about a women's band." Jane smiled. "You know the Indian saying, 'Say money, and a corpse will rise.' "

"I know, I know, but if the women could say, 'We don't get paid. God supplies our needs. We come because we love God and you!' "

"That would be wonderful." Jane stopped her work and turned to Amy. "The Indians would really listen and believe such a messenger. But Amy, face facts, it can never happen."

Amy answered,

```
┌─────────────┐   1. "I guess you are right."
│   GUESS     │   2. "You know the Indians better than I."
└─────────────┘   3. "With God all things are possible."
```

" 'With God all things are possible,' " Amy quoted. "I'm going to pray for God to give us a band of consecrated women."

Amy continued helping the Walkers, but she never forgot to pray for a group of women to travel with her. Jane and Walker prayed, too, though Walker admitted, "My faith is weak. I always pay my men when they work full time. How could they otherwise support their families, buy food, live?"

Two years later in July 1897, Amy moved with the Walkers to a new place. Here in Pannaivilai Amy found

```
┌─────────────┐   1. a native church.
│   GUESS     │   2. a Sunday school teacher.
└─────────────┘   3. many enemies.
```

"I'm so glad there is a church here already," she said. Soon she became acquainted with one of the Sunday school teachers, Ponnammal.

"Why are you so sad?" Amy asked, seeing the pain in Ponnammal's eyes.

"Oh, Musal Missi," the young woman answered. "I will tell you one day."

The church members called Amy *Musal,* which means

GUESS

1. the dog.
2. the hare.
3. the lion.

They called her *Musal* because she always moved so quickly, like a hare.

As soon as possible Amy visited Ponnammal in her home. "Could we go for a walk in the woods?" Ponnammal questioned. Amy agreed.

After a brisk walk, Amy sat down on a fallen tree and asked again, "Why are you so sad?"

The woods were quiet. The wind was still. After several moments the woman spoke slowly. "You see, Missi, my husband is dead, and I live with his parents." Ponnammal finally sat beside her on the log.

"His parents resent the food I eat. They would chase me away if it were not for my son—their grandson—you understand."

Amy tried to find a bright spot in this. "But your son must be a comfort."

"No, Missi, they have

GUESS

1. hidden him."
2. turned him against me."
3. tied him up."

As Ponnammal spoke, Amy began to see that the young mother was only a household drudge.

"My son has been turned against me. My only comfort is Jesus," Ponnammal declared. "I love Him better than life and am so happy I can teach my Sunday school class. My only desire is to work for the Lord. I do wish there were something I could do."

Amy fell on her knees beside the tree. "Oh, God, thank You for Ponnammal. Use her, Jesus, use her." Together they prayed for a long time.

When they rose to their feet and started to walk back, Amy told Ponnammal of her dream of a band of Indian sisters. Ponnammal quickly

GUESS

1. volunteered.
2. backed away.
3. promised to pray.

Ponnammal volunteered to be the first of the band of sisters. Leyal, the pastor's daughter, was second, and a one-armed woman called Pearl begged to go with Amy on the trips, also. Slowly the group grew.

They traveled in a wagon called a bandy, pulled by

GUESS

1. horses.
2. oxen.
3. bullocks.

Bullocks pulled the heavy wagon of supplies, sleeping gear, and women. They would camp near a village. Every morning they visited in the homes and talked to everyone who would listen. At noon they

GUESS

1. worshiped the sun.
2. ate dinner together.
3. studied the Bible.

They ate dinner and studied the Bible at noon. Later they again visited in homes and invited everyone to the afternoon meeting. Amy usually started the meeting by the village well. She sang and talked about Jesus. Then the women spoke, one after the other. Amy noticed that the Indian people

| GUESS |
1. were more interested in her.
2. seemed to believe the native women.
3. rejected all mention of Christ.

"They believe what the Indian women tell them," Amy observed.

When the question of money came up, Ponnammal spoke.

| GUESS |
1. "God supplies our needs."
2. "Money falls from heaven."
3. "Strangers share with us."

Ponnammal explained how God supplied whatever they needed. "People give us food, clothing, or shelter. The people love us. They cannot love without giving," she said.

"But why do you deny yourselves?" the Indians cried.

"Because we love you, Jesus loves you, and we love Jesus."

Amy saw that the Indian listeners understood at last.

The women said, "Let's give ourselves a name. Let's call ourselves

| GUESS |
1. the Sisters' Band."
2. the Starry Cluster."
3. the Women's Group."

They named themselves the Starry Cluster. Those who had been Hindu wanted to change their names also, now that they were Christians. Ponnammal changed her name to *Golden*. She said, "It is because, in the Indian language, Golden is one who never turns back—one who always marches forward."

Amy promised no salaries, but she did give them gifts of money—*batta*, she called it.

One morning they knocked at the Walkers' door, asked for Amy, and demanded

1. more money.

GUESS

2. less money.

3. no money.

The women marched to the dining room table and poured all the money into a pile. "We don't need it, and we don't want it," they said. "If we get money, even if it is a gift, the people will misunderstand."

Amy hugged them all. "God bless you, dear sisters!"

The Starry Cluster grew so large that Amy divided the group. She left half of the women in Pannaivilai. The other half of the group moved with Amy across the river. Golden said, "I go where you go, Amy." They left the Walkers with tears, but everyone believed that two groups could reach more people.

One day as the Starry Cluster set out in the bandy, a husband of one of the members walked beside the wagon. "You know," he said, "if you really loved Jesus, you wouldn't be wearing all that jewelry." The young woman removed her chains and beads, the multitudinous bracelets, and the nose and earrings. They left the husband standing in the middle of the road

GUESS

1. laden down with gold.

2. holding a bag.

3. waving good-bye.

Laden down with jewelry, the husband stared after the bandy. He murmured, "I never dreamed she loved Christ that much."

Amy said to the young wife,

GUESS

1. "Good for you."

2. "Jesus is pleased."

3. nothing.

Amy said nothing, knowing the importance of jewelry to Indian women. All the women thought about their jewelry. Jewels were a married woman's dowry, evidence of her husband's position, caste, and wealth. No woman in India went anywhere without her jewels.

During the journey the women whispered among themselves,

GUESS	1. "Can I give up *my* jewels?" 2. "Does Christ mean more than jewelry?" 3. "Jewels are more beautiful than Jesus."

Each woman examined herself. "Can I give up *my* jewels?"

When they reached their destination, all the women removed their jewels.

"I would have loved my Savior more," Golden said, "if I had loved my jewels less."

"With this last vanity removed, nothing can stop our work for Jesus," Amy said, not knowing the difficulties that lay ahead.

9

The Child-Catching Missi

Amy celebrated her twenty-ninth birthday with her Indian "sisters." Together they traveled to

```
GUESS
```
1. the mountains.
2. the plains.
3. the valleys.

Amy wrote a letter to her mother: "During the hot dry season, we go to the mountains. When the weather cools, we return again to the valleys. Everywhere we give the gospel to hungry Indians. My years here are happy with these Christian helpers. Some women of the Starry Cluster stay away from their homes

```
GUESS
```
1. a few weeks.
2. a few months.
3. always.

"Some women stay with me permanently. Others can only stay for a few weeks each year, because of home duties. I accept whatever time they can give. Oh, Mother, I thank you for your prayers.

Always remember I love my family."

Gradually Amy saw that the Indians preferred to hear

GUESS

1. her testimony.
2. their own people.
3. nothing.

"Since the adults seem to prefer to hear their own people," Amy decided, "I'll hold children's meetings."

So while the adults met on one side of the village well, Amy gathered the children around her on the far side. Soon there were more children than adults, because

GUESS

1. all castes came.
2. the lower castes came.
3. the outcasts came.

The children came to the meetings regardless of caste. Some came knowing that they would receive beatings at home afterward.

"What kind of spell does she put over the children, that they love her so?" the parents marveled. "She must use a power to drug them, so that they long to be near her." They gave Amy a new name: "The Child-Catching Missi."

Some parents threatened to

GUESS

1. beat Amy.
2. drug Amy.
3. murder Amy.

Amy ignored the threats of murder. "God will protect me," she said.

One warm night when Amy was safe in her little home, she heard

1. scratching at her door.

72

GUESS

2. bells ringing.
3. feet marching.

She heard a scratching at her door.

"Refuge! Refuge!" a desperate voice called. When Amy opened the door, a sixteen-year-old girl of the goldsmith caste stumbled inside.

"Why are you here?" Amy asked.

"Oh, Amma [Mother], I cannot live a Christian life at home. When you came to our village and told us of the Christ who died for us, I believed." The girl could not go on because of her deep sobs.

Amy put her arms around the girl and cried also. "When you hurt, dear, I hurt, too," Amy said.

The girl wanted to

GUESS

1. live with Amy.
2. run away.
3. get married.

"Let me live with you!" the girl pleaded.

"I cannot promise you a home," Amy said, "but come inside for the night." Golden gave up her bedroom on the second floor and slept at the bottom of the stairs.

In the morning the girl told them of being forced to take part in Hindu worship. "Oh, Amma, I cannot do it. I know Jesus is not pleased."

They had finished breakfast and had Bible reading, when

GUESS

1. the relatives pounded on the door.
2. the police arrived.
3. the Hindu holy men came.

Amy opened the door and faced the angry relatives.

"Release her at once!" they demanded and started to push inside.

Amy put her arms across the doorway. "Be quiet, and we will

talk about this," she said in a soothing voice.

"How have you bewitched our daughter?" the parents cried.

"I've done nothing," Amy answered. "If your daughter wishes to go with you, she is free to do so."

That quieted the crowd, and Amy called the young woman to her side. "You know the law of India. A sixteen-year-old person may live where she chooses." Amy turned to the girl. "Where do you wish to live?" she asked.

The girl answered,

GUESS

1. "I'll go with my relatives."
2. "I wish to stay with you."
3. "I want to live with my parents."

To the relatives' dismay, the girl told them, "I cannot go with you. Jesus is my Savior, and I wish to stay here where I can worship Him." Before the relatives could recover from their shock, the girl

GUESS

1. ran away.
2. slipped away to the upstairs room.
3. slammed the door.

After her speech the young woman slipped away to her upstairs room. Amy faced the relatives alone.

"What have you done? We raised our daughter to be a true Hindu. Why did you come with your devil words?" Torrents of abusive speech fell on Amy's head.

She answered,

GUESS

1. "I'm sorry."
2. "Don't be angry."
3. "You know the law."

Amy only reminded them of the Indian laws. Then she gently shut and locked the door.

74

For hours the girl's relatives

```
┌─────────────┐   1. beat on the door.
│             │   2. milled around the house.
│   GUESS     │   3. shouted threats.
│             │
└─────────────┘
```

Amy held the young lady in her arms, as the relatives milled around the house. She felt the girl's sobs and trembled with her. Together they waited through the long hours. Finally, the relatives

```
┌─────────────┐   1. broke down the door.
│             │   2. went away.
│   GUESS     │   3. called the police.
│             │
└─────────────┘
```

Finally the relatives went away, after pronouncing curses and threats.

The next Sunday Amy took the girl with her to the Christian church. The preacher said, "We praise you for your firm stand for Christ." The members also admired the young girl's beauty. A local poet attending the meeting said, "I know you no longer want your Hindu name, now that you are baptized. Let me give you a name that becomes your courage—*Jewel of Victory*."

Victory went with the Starry Cluster and told Bible stories to the very small children. Amy was

```
┌─────────────┐   1. grateful for the help.
│             │   2. afraid Victory might be snatched away.
│   GUESS     │   3. sure that Victory would be a great teacher.
│             │
└─────────────┘
```

Amy watched Jewel of Victory with the little children and prayed to God, "Make of her a great teacher." She wrote letters to the Keswick Committee, telling of the girl's dedication to Christ and her need for a home. The Committee answered,

1. "We can't afford to support her."

GUESS
2. "Send her back."
3. "Don't worry about money."

The D.O.M. assured Amy that God would provide the needs for a home for all who came.

Less than six months later, another girl came to Amy's house in the night. Both Victory and Amy heard the scratching on the door.

"Don't answer it—it may be my relatives," Victory warned.

"And it may be someone in trouble," Amy reminded her. Together they crept downstairs and listened.

"Let me in, oh, please, Amma!" Amy flung open the door and pulled inside a dark form, wet with perspiration. Together, she and Victory dried the young woman with towels. They gave her something to eat and drink, comforting her with soothing words.

Finally, the girl was able to talk. "I've been running all night. Oh, Amma, I heard you tell of the Christ who loves us, when you were in my village. But I couldn't come then. I

GUESS
1. was not sixteen."
2. was held in bondage."
3. loved the Hindu religion."

"I wanted to raise my hand to tell you I asked Jesus to come into my heart, but I was afraid. My family is of a high caste and would kill me before they would let me go."

"But you have come now, praise the Lord," Victory told her. "Just as I came."

"Yes, I waited, telling no one I was a Jesus believer until my birthday. Today, at last, I am free to run away." The two girls hugged.

Amy braced herself to face relatives once more.

"There is nothing your people can say that has not been said. And better yet, there is nothing they can do, since you are sixteen." Amy comforted the girl and sent her off to bed with Jewel of Victory.

When the poet met the second young lady at church the next Sunday, he grinned.

"Another Jewel for Jesus, I believe." He named her

| GUESS |

1. "Jewel for Jesus."
2. "Jewel of Life."
3. "Jewel of Love."

He named her *Jewel of Life*. She, too, eventually became a member of the Starry Cluster.

Amy laughed. "Two Jewels for Jesus' crown!" Then looking toward heaven she said, "What will become of them?"

10

Arulai

One Sunday in church, Amy felt someone nestle down beside her. As Amy looked into the eyes of a beautiful little girl, her heart was touched and love for this child flooded through her. They held hands for the remainder of the service.

After church Amy prepared to walk back over the swinging bridge and down the tree-lined dirt road to her house. The girl walked beside her.

"Take me home with you," she pleaded.

"What's your name?"

"Arulai."

"That's a pretty name. Where is your mother?"

"You are my Amma! I love you and have no other mother. Only a father."

"Why don't you stay with him?"

Arulai stopped and began to sob.

"There, there." Amy paused, sat on a large rock, and took the child into her arms. "You can tell me," she said, stroking the girl's hair.

When Arulai finally controlled herself, she lifted her face to Amy's and burst out, "I always dreaded it. I had to let him touch me, but I hated it."

As she sobbed once more, Amy rocked back and forth, saying gently,

GUESS	1. "I know it hurts."
	2. "I hurt with you."
	3. "Stop crying."

"I hurt with you," she told the child.

"He expects me to tell no one, to act as though nothing happened, like nothing hurts inside. But, Amma, it does, it does." Again Arulai broke down. Amy patted the child until she was quiet.

"Come, we must be on our way. Golden will have dinner ready and will wonder where I am."

As they walked, Amy asked more questions. "How old are you?"

"Eleven."

"Do you always have enough to eat?"

"Yes."

"Does your father beat you?"

"Sometimes. Not when I 'cooperate,' as he says."

"Do you love Jesus?"

"I don't know Him. The only Jesus I know is what I see in your eyes. I saw it when you spoke in my village. I see it now."

Amy said,

GUESS	1. "I can tell you of Jesus."
	2. "That's not being saved."
	3. "That won't make you a Christian."

Amy smiled. "I can tell you all about the Savior after we have had our dinner."

They walked up the path, and Golden greeted them. "We have plenty of dinner for all, especially for one hungry-looking little girl. Do come in."

Arulai's relatives came in large numbers the next day, chanting, raving, and threatening. They beat on the door, and Amy finally opened it. But Amy

GUESS	1. refused to give Arulai to them.
	2. let them take Arulai.

79

3. couldn't stop them.

The relatives shouted, "She's only eleven, and you know the law of India."

This time Amy was helpless. She pleaded with the aunts and uncles. "I do know the law, and I can't stop you, but don't hand her over to her father!"

The relatives led Arulai away.

Amy never forgot the look Arulai gave her. "She's like a wild beast caught in a trap." Amy choked. "Oh, why am I so helpless?"

For eight months Amy prayed and mourned. She saw Christians, especially children, beaten and prevented from attending her meetings. One father threatened to throw pepper in his son's eyes if he did not renounce his faith in Christ. Another sent his son away to the mountains.

Even members of the Starry Cluster suffered. One young woman, who had tossed away her jewels and had powerfully spoken for Christ, suddenly seemed to care for nothing. Amy guessed she

GUESS	1. had been drugged.
	2. was sick.
	3. had been poisoned.

"The girl must have been poisoned, for she babbles like an idiot." Amy wept. "She will never be the same again."

Amy would awaken suddenly, night after night. She would think,

GUESS	1. "Arulai has come back."
	2. "A robber is here."
	3. "A runaway has come."

Each time, she hurried from her bed, but Arulai was not in the house, and no robber or runaway appeared. Amy worried as she went back to her room. "It's been eight months, and I still have this nightmare." She sighed.

One Sunday morning she prayed in her heart, *Give me some*

token for good, dear Lord! Some people say that Arulai has turned against Christ. That's a lie! Oh, God, help me!

As Amy pushed back the sun blind to the veranda that morning, she was astonished to see

GUESS

1. Jewel of Victory.
2. Jewel of Life.
3. Arulai.

Before Amy's delighted eyes, Arulai stepped onto the veranda. Amy threw open the door and took her into her arms. It was a moment before she realized something was wrong, and she placed Arulai on a couch. "She used her last strength to get here," Amy said. She stared at the dark bruises on the girl's neck and arms.

Golden soon had Arulai's feet in hot water and a cold towel on her forehead. Amy, usually in command, stood helpless, as though stunned. She sprang to life, however, when Arulai opened her eyes.

"Who hurt you?" she cried. "What happened?"

"Father—he beat me." Slowly Arulai spoke as though she were in a stupor. "He tied me to a post in the loft. He gave me poison."

At the word *poison*, Amy warmed milk and forced it down Arulai's throat. She pushed her fingers as far into her mouth as possible and turned her on her stomach.

Soon the milk came up, and with it a green substance. Amy put the child to bed and nursed her day and night. Golden ran several miles for a doctor, who told them, "Arulai would have died if you had not rid her of most of the poison. She is still a very sick girl. Keep her in bed."

Arulai's father came the next day. He said, "I'll take Arulai away."

Amy responded,

GUESS

1. "She's too sick to move."
2. "Let her stay awhile."
3. "Please don't take her!"

Amy said, "Arulai is too sick to move."

81

The man looked at Arulai, then at Amy. Slowly he agreed and walked away, saying, "I'll be back for her in a few days."

"I wish he would get in trouble for what he did," Arulai said. "My aunt always blames me for letting him touch me. How am I supposed to stop him?"

"My dear child," Amy comforted her, "you are not to blame! Jesus would never blame you."

"That's what I tell myself, but sometimes I

GUESS
1. blame myself anyway."
2. ask Jesus to forgive me."
3. hate my father."

"You can't blame yourself. There is nothing to forgive, my dear. You are the victim." Amy tried to take the guilt away but realized only Christ could do that.

"Don't let me go back to the dark, please, Lord," Amy heard Arulai pray. "Oh, let me live in the light!"

Amy's heart was torn, and she thought of a plan to

GUESS
1. make the father depart.
2. disgrace the father.
3. punish the father.

Amy didn't try to punish or disgrace Arulai's father. "Only let him leave Arulai in my care," she prayed to Jesus.

After a week, the father returned and found Arulai feeling much better. "I'll take her home now," he stated.

"The Indian law does not allow murder, not even of your daughter." Amy looked the father squarely in the eyes. "You gave her poison. You tied her to a post in a loft." Amy glared. "You beat her and left her to die." Amy held him spellbound with her charges. "Do—you—wish—me—to—go—on?" She pointed her finger in his face. "Leave Arulai here, and I will say no more."

Amy's eyes never left those of the father, until he

1. hit her.

82

"You gave her poison."

GUESS
2. grabbed his daughter.
3. left the house.

The man turned on his heel and slowly left the house.

The women of the Starry Cluster celebrated. "How did you dare to overpower a man of India?" they marveled.

"Thank You, Jesus, for letting me live in the light!" Arulai cried. "And thank you, Missi Ammal."

A few days later, Amy received a letter from a book publisher. "Please write a book of your experiences in India, as you wrote of Japan," they requested.

Later Amy wrote to her mother: "I took time from work to write a book. I wrote of the converts who withstood persecution. Also, I wrote of those who turned back, unable to overcome. I included tales of incest, greed, dishonesty, as well as answers to prayer. And I even wrote of my deepest fears, that I'm afraid temple children are sexually abused. I named my book *Things As They Are*. Pray, dear mother, that God will use this book to wake up Christians."

The publishers

GUESS
1. printed Amy's book.
2. rejected Amy's book.
3. ignored Amy's book.

The publishers said, "We cannot print such a book showing the dark side of life. Write happy endings, not this!"

Amy

GUESS
1. wrote a happy book.
2. never wrote again.
3. put the book in a drawer.

Amy put the book in a drawer and forgot about it.

11

Dohnavur

For three years Amy

GUESS

1. held children's meetings.
2. feared Arulai's father.
3. worked with the Starry Cluster.

Amy, along with the Starry Cluster, held meetings from village to village. Everywhere Amy went, she took Arulai.

By the time Arulai was fourteen, she always knew what Amy would want. "Here is your tea, Amma," she would say. Or, "Let me fold down your bed." Together they shared their dreams.

One evening when Amy entered their bedroom, she found Arulai in tears because she

GUESS

1. hated her father.
2. blamed herself.
3. buried her feelings.

"I still feel like I'm to blame. I hate him," Arulai sobbed. "How could he do that to me?"

"No, no," Amy comforted.

"I can say it's not my fault. You can say it, too, but way down I still feel guilty."

"Please don't torture yourself. Jesus has washed all your sins away. You know that." Amy tried to comfort her.

"I guess it's something that will be there the rest of my life." Arulai wiped her eyes.

"Pray for victory. The Bible promises that if you ask for anything in His name, it can happen. Ask, my dear. Promise!"

"I promise I'll ask God for peace, even though I still hurt." Arulai looked into Amy's eyes a long time. "I do still hurt, Amma."

For some time they clung together. Then gently they both slipped to the floor and prayed.

One morning in 1899, Amy had company.

GUESS	1. Jewel of Victory.
	2. Jewel of Life.
	3. Walker.

Walker was full of news.

"Come in for a cup of tea," Amy invited. "Where is Jane?"

"She's packing."

"Packing!" Amy cried. "Where is she going?"

"That's my news." Walker laughed. "We are moving to Dohnavur, at least for a time."

"Why? Here, come into the kitchen. Have a chair, and let's talk." Amy motioned to Arulai.

Arulai understood and set out the cups and teapot. She started the water boiling and greeted Walker. Soon she filled the teapot and left the friends together.

"What a lovely young lady she is," Walker remarked.

Amy answered, "Oh, she's

GUESS	1. healing."
	2. still scared."
	3. still hurting."

86

"Her father has left many scars, but Jesus is healing them one by one. I fear sometimes that her father might come for her. She isn't sixteen yet, you know." Amy interrupted herself. "But, come now—you are comfortable—tell me the news. Why are you moving?"

"I have been asked to teach at a school in Dohnavur."

"Isn't that some distance away? I have heard good things about that school. German missionaries are in charge, right?"

"That's right. About seventy-five years ago, Count Dohna came to India. He founded a church, a school, and you might say, a village for converts to Christianity."

"What became of them?" Amy inquired.

"For some years after the Count died, the German mission sent workers, but now they have no one to send. They have asked me to teach the few students who remain."

"Isn't it dry in that part of the country?"

"Yes, some even call it a desert, but they have plenty of water, I understand."

"They have a lake?"

"No."

"A river, then?"

"No. No one knows why, but everywhere they dig, they find water."

"Does Jane want to go?"

"She will be happy to go if

GUESS

1. you go with us."
2. the Indian brothers continue working here."
3. we have a nice house."

Walker explained, "Jane and I both want you to go with us." Amy

GUESS

1. fainted.
2. said, "Oh, no."
3. considered the idea.

Once Amy recovered from the shock, she and Walker discussed the good and bad things about the move.

Gradually a sparkle gleamed in Amy's eyes. "You know, I've had a dream for some time of an orphanage. I've taken in over a dozen runaways already, and we can hardly handle any more. Could this be God's provision?"

Now Walker objected.

GUESS	1. "You can't tend children."
	2. "You can't give up your Christian work."
	3. "You musn't tie yourself down."

Walker objected. "You can't give up your Christian work to tend babies!"

"Who said bringing up children in the faith is not Christian work?" Amy's eyes blazed. "I feel it is God's will. Yes, I'll go!"

Walker was silent. He had never seen Amy so sure of anything before.

"Well." Walker swallowed.

GUESS	1. "God will be pleased."
	2. "Jane will be pleased."
	3. "I'll never approve."

"Jane will be pleased," Walker admitted. "I'll write to the German mission about an orphanage." He and Amy prayed. Then Walker turned to go.

"Can't you accept new ideas?" Amy called after him.

Once the Starry Cluster learned of the decision, some of the band said, "We can carry on the work here." But others said,

GUESS	1. "We quit."
	2. "We will never forgive you."
	3. "We are going with the Musal Missi."

Golden decided, "Where you go, I go."

Jewel of Victory and Jewel of Life, now nineteen years old, also said, "We'll go." Arulai

```
┌─────────────┐   1. decided to go back to her father.
│   GUESS     │   2. ran away.
└─────────────┘   3. decided to go with Amy.
```

"Amma!" Arulai cried. "I go with you. I do, I do!"

"We will work in the nearby villages and Dohnavur until we hear from the German mission about the orphanage," Amy cautioned those who agreed to move. As they packed for the trip, Amy suggested, "Do not take everything until we are sure we will stay."

The group set out on the long trip full of questions. During the many days of travel, the land about them changed from green to brown.

At last Amy glimpsed the mission buildings. She noticed dry sand everywhere and the blazing sun overhead. The weary women of the Starry Cluster thankfully ran forward. Amy and Jane hugged each other as they surveyed the mission compound, for

```
┌─────────────┐   1. the people were of the palmyra climbers caste.
│   GUESS     │   2. there were several empty buildings.
└─────────────┘   3. the trees and shrubs abounded.
```

"What great buildings in such good condition! Plenty of housing for everyone," Amy rejoiced. "Plenty of room for an orphanage."

"And look at the trees and shrubs growing in this sand," Jane added.

Amy's quarters included a parlor of her own facing west. "Look, Arulai, see the mountains. They are the southernmost peaks of the Western Ghauts. See that double-headed mountain? That's called

```
┌─────────────┐   1. the Twins."
│   GUESS     │   2. the Holy Watchman."
└─────────────┘   3. the Two Heads."
```

"The mountain is called the Holy Watchman. I think it is watching over Dohnavur. Everything's been ready, just waiting for us to come."

Together, with arms entwined, the two gazed over the hot dusty plains to the snow-capped peak.

"We are safe at last," Arulai cried.

Amy turned and looked into her eyes. "A few months ago, I hardly knew of this place, and now I feel I'm safe. I'm home! Thank You, Lord Jesus!"

"And Father will never find me here!" Arulai added.

12

The Orphanage

One morning in early 1900, Walker knocked on Amy's door. "Your letter from the German mission has arrived after all these months," he called.

"Oh, what does it say?" Amy asked. She stepped outside and took the letter. She held it in her hand unopened.

"Read it and find out." Walker laughed. "Patting it and turning it over and over will never tell you anything."

"I'm afraid to find out."

"Then we will never know!"

"Will you never stop teasing me?" Amy asked, as she opened the letter. She read, "We will

	1. not allow an orphanage."
GUESS	2. sell you land for an orphanage."
	3. build an orphanage for you."

The Germans stated, "We will gladly sell land to a Christian organization. In the meantime, use the existing buildings for an orphanage."

Amy wailed, "Oh, but we have

GUESS

1. no organization."
2. no money."
3. no builders."

"But the Church of England Society would never buy land. They refused to give us money for the runaways. They do not approve of an orphanage. Oh, what can we do, Walker?"

"What did you expect they would say, Amy?" Walker patted her shoulder. "Maybe you had better pray about it. Are you sure this is God's will?"

Amy pulled away. "I will pray, sir. You may be sure of that." Amy followed Walker with her eyes, as he hurried to his classroom. "He's a real man of God. But he simply does not see the need for an orphanage." She shook her head sadly.

Then without warning, visitors came from England—Ella Crossley and Mary Hatch. The sight of friendly faces and good news of Mother, Ethel, and Ava made Amy rejoice.

"How nice of you to come! You are a breath from home," Amy said. She took them along with the Starry Cluster when they visited the villages.

"You may as well see things as they are," Amy said.

Mary and Ella spoke with the women of the Starry Cluster about

GUESS

1. their lives.
2. their hopes.
3. their fights.

Mary and Ella wanted to know everything of the Indian women's lives and hopes. They talked for a long time with Amy interpreting. When Arulai and Jewel of Victory joined the conversation, they, too, revealed their secrets. After two weeks of visiting, the two women said to Amy, "We wish

GUESS

1. the folks at home knew of the work."
2. you had an organization."
3. you would write a book."

The women from England said, "We wish most of all that you would write a book."

"But I already wrote a book," Amy objected. "I called it *Things As They Are,* and the publishers wanted me to tell only of the 'nice' things that happen. They wanted me to say that a woman of the Starry Cluster recovered from poison, when she did not. She is feeble-minded to this day. I won't change facts to make a happy ending. I won't!"

Mary and Ella looked stunned. "Let us see the book," they insisted. After reading it, they said,

GUESS	1. "Let us take it."
	2. "We will try to find a publisher."
	3. "People have a right to know."

"If you let us take it," Mary and Ella said, "we will try to find an open-minded publisher. We promise."

"Well, for sure, it's doing no one any good in the drawer," Amy agreed.

Ella added, "I've been taking pictures since I've been here. Why can't they be included in the book?"

"Or course." Then Amy laughed. "Did you know the Indians call you the Picture-Catching Missi Ammal?"

As they bade Amy good-bye, Mary and Ella reminded her, "Think about an organization, Amy. You could call it 'The Fellowship.' We could tell people about it. God might direct some of them to send money for the orphanages. Think about it, Amy."

Amy

GUESS	1. forgot about the orphanage.
	2. prayed.
	3. felt it was hopeless.

"Oh, Lord, if it be possible, raise up an orphanage," Amy prayed.

The visitors were hardly gone when a frightened woman rushed up to Amy after a village meeting.

93

"Here, take my baby girl. Take her quick. I'd rather you have her than the temple women." She thrust the infant into Amy's arms and disappeared.

Amy said,

GUESS

1. "I can't take care of a *baby*."
2. "Give her to the temple."
3. "I'll love the wee one."

Amy stood still for some time. Then she looked down at the sleeping infant. "I'll love you, little one, that I will."

When they returned from the village to Dohnavur, Amy announced to the Starry Cluster, "The time has come to start the orphans' home. We have one building that is not being used. I'll go back to Pannaivilai and get the children who are still there with Mrs. Hopwood."

She said, "Again it is time to divide the Starry Cluster. Some of you may want to

GUESS

1. work in the orphanage."
2. leave the work."
3. work in the villages."

"While I'm gone, pray about it," Amy told them. "God will surely show you if He wants you to work in the orphanage or in the villages."

"Oh, I know I want to work with the children," Golden decided. "Let me take the baby."

Amy left Dohnavur for Pannaivilai the first of March, 1901. "I need a few days of rest before packing the things I left behind," she said.

After the long trip, friends made her comfortable. "You are spoiling me," Amy said after a few days of rest.

At 6:30 A.M. on the morning of March 7, Amy and her hostess were having prayer when a knock came at the door.

A woman stepped inside with a very small girl, who looked about seven years old. The girl

GUESS	1. held to the woman's skirts.
	2. stared with big eyes.
	3. ran to Amy.

The little girl raced to Amy. "Are you the Child-Catching Missi Ammal?" she cried.

"They call me that."

"Then catch me, please," the child pleaded, her big eyes full of tears.

Amy drew her onto her lap and kissed her.

"My mother used to kiss me like this," the child said. "Who is this person who kisses like my mother?"

Amy looked into the child's enormous eyes. Without words, Amy hugged this new daughter. The child snuggled in her arms. "Mother," she said, "you are my Ammal!"

The hostess invited the woman to sit with them and asked, "Who are you?"

"I attend the native Christian church. I've seen you and the Musal Missi there several times," the woman explained.

"What of the child?"

"That's why I came. Before dark last night, I noticed her on the steps of the church and asked about her." The woman looked at the child sitting so contentedly on Amy's lap. "She said she was looking for the Child-Catching Missi Ammal. I asked her why, and she began to cry. So I took her home with me, it being so late."

Amy broke in, "Did she ever say why?"

"No, but I could see she was afraid, so I

GUESS	1. forced her to tell."
	2. offered her food."
	3. put her to bed."

The woman said, "Poor little thing, I could see she was hungry, but though I offered her food, she couldn't eat at my house, she being of a higher caste, you understand. When she woke this morning, I brought her here. That's all I know."

Suddenly the woman stood up and left, as though afraid.

"She must eat now," the hostess suggested, looking at the

child. She at once brought rice and eggs.

Amy gave the girl a bath and washed her hair and clothes. After rolling the clothes in a towel, she shook them out and gave them back to the child. "They will soon dry in this heat," she said.

"There, you look like a beauty." Amy nodded with satisfaction.

"Oh, they always said I was pretty." The girl looked up into Amy's eyes.

"Who?" Amy held her breath.

The child answered,

```
+-----------+
|           |   1. "The temple women."
|  GUESS    |   2. "The holy men."
|           |   3. "My mother."
+-----------+
```

The child answered, "The temple women." She then said, "My mother sold me to the temple to be married to the god, but I ran away, back to my mother." The child sobbed. "But she took my arms from around her neck and gave me back to the temple women when they came."

"Did they punish you?" Amy inquired.

"Yes, they burned my arms—see!" She showed the deep scars on her arms. "They told me they would burn me all over if I ran away again." Amy sat in silence, until the child continued. "So I learned the dances, and how to move my body to please the men," she whispered softly, as she hid her face in the folds of Amy's dress. Amy could hardly hear her.

"But you did run away again," Amy prompted.

"Yes, I heard of the mother who catches children, so I came to find you!" The girl broke into tears again.

Amy asked, "What is your name, dear one?"

The child answered,

```
+-----------+
|           |   1. "Tutic."
|  GUESS    |   2. "Preena."
|           |   3. "Corin."
+-----------+
```

"My name is Preena. You will keep me, won't you?"

Amy held her very tightly. She didn't know what to say.

Oh, God, You have sent her to me. Please let me keep her, Amy prayed.

13

Who Believes?

Later that same day, Walker and the Indian pastor visited Amy. She told them about Preena. Walker insisted, "You can't take the word of a seven-year-old child!"

"No, no," the pastor said. "You must obey the law. You must learn the facts."

"And who is going to tell the facts, sir?" Amy demanded. "I've always suspected that the temple children were sexually abused. But no one would tell me."

"That's true," the pastor agreed. "They always turn away if I ask about the practice, but the fact is that our church wants no trouble with the law."

"Do you understand, Amy?" Walker pleaded.

GUESS	1. "Preena is only one child." 2. "Think of the others." 3. "Do you want to endanger all?"

The reasonable tone and the logic of Walker's words upset Amy. She said,

1. "Preena is only one."

GUESS	2. "But she called for me." 3. "But she ran to me."

Amy's eyes blazed. "She ran to me for help, and I'll do everything I can for this precious child. I, for one, believe her story."

"Very well," the pastor agreed. "We will send word by messenger to the temple on the Great Lake to verify her story. Once we know the facts, we will do what we can to save her."

Amy was silent, but in her heart she raved, "And you'll send her back! I must do something myself."

Amy packed her things and arranged with her helper Mrs. Hopwood to move the other children to Dohnavur. Preena followed at Amy's heels all day. Amy did not tell her

GUESS	1. she was to go back. 2. she couldn't go with them. 3. the law would not help.

Amy waited. She could not tell Preena that the law would not protect her.

As the missionaries were loading their things into wagons the next day, the women from the temple arrived. Their saris were white silk, their hair neat and clean. Their knock on the front door was calm enough. When Amy confronted them, they said sweetly,

GUESS	1. "We are servants of the gods." 2. "We come from heaven." 3. "The child Preena is ours."

"The child is ours," they said sweetly, but their jaws were firm.

"By what right do you claim her?" Amy asked, mocking their sweet voices.

"Her mother sold her to us, as she was unable to care for her." They spoke politely and obviously expected Amy to give up the child.

"By what right do you claim her?"

"Do you have the certificate of sale?" Amy inquired.
This question

GUESS

1. surprised the women.
2. angered them.
3. worried them.

Suddenly the politeness vanished. "Who are you to question us, the servants of the gods?" They spat in anger.

"I am a servant of the one true God," Amy answered, pulling herself up to her full height. "The child does not wish to go with you."

Preena ran to a closet to hide. She cried, "Don't let them take me, Amma. Please!"

The women heard the cry and demanded, "Let us in at once!"

When Amy resisted, they tried to

GUESS

1. push open the door.
2. search the house.
3. go home.

Amy's eyes flashed fire. She felt as though the very strength of God was in her. "Hold back!" she cried, when the temple women started to push inside. She held up her arms to bar the door. Preena crept from the closet to peep around her skirts.

As though hypnotized, the women withdrew. "We will tell her mother you stole her. She will come and demand the child. You will suffer at the hands of the law. See if you don't!"

"Very well." Amy rose on her toes, almost filling the small doorway. "When her mother comes, I'll give the child to her. That is the law, and I will obey."

The temple women

GUESS

1. went away.
2. started to fight.
3. snarled and spit.

Snarling and spitting, the temple women went off toward the lake.

Preena peered out the doorway at their backs. "Amma, you're brave," she said, as she clung to Amy. "I'll stay with you always."

Amy held Preena tightly. "Let us pray it is so." The two were on their knees when Walker came in.

"I heard the temple women went away." He smiled. "You must have overpowered them."

"No," Amy answered, "God delivered us from them. If the mother ever comes here, she won't find us, for we leave for Dohnavur early in the morning."

"If she makes the long journey to Dohnavur," Walker cautioned, "we will have to deal with the problem."

"But she won't," Amy responded.

The mother

GUESS

1. never came.
2. went to Dohnavur.
3. obeyed the temple women.

Amy was right. The mother never came to Dohnavur.

Once the missionaries and children arrived safely in Dohnavur, Arulai and Preena became like sisters. They told each other their secrets. It was Arulai who persuaded Preena to tell Amy the details about what went on in the temples.

Amy managed to remain calm while Preena explained. "The priests give us to the men who come to the temple."

Later Amy raved to her friend Golden,

GUESS

1. "Something must be done!"
2. "I must do something!"
3. "We are helpless!"

Amy ranted, "If these things are so, something must be done!"

"Yes, you must do something," Golden agreed. "But what?"

Amy carried that question in her mind for days. "But what? What can I do?"

She arranged the children's rooms. "This must have been a dormitory when the German count was here," she decided. "But it can be made cheerful for the children."

She and Golden cleaned one of the rooms for a nursery. While they worked, they talked. "How can parents give up their children?" Amy asked.

Golden answered, "The parents

| GUESS |

1. may be ill."
2. may be separated."
3. may be dead."

"It happens, sometimes, the parents may be ill and unable to care for a baby, so they give her away. Or it may be they need money so desperately for food that they sell the child."

Amy dropped her bucket, flung her mop on the floor, and raised her hands. "I know what I can do! I'll

| GUESS |

1. write a book."
2. go to the government."
3. preach a sermon."

"I'll write a book!" Amy declared. As quickly as possible, she did so. She titled it *Lotus Buds*. Some things she felt were unprintable. Still, she wrote more than people wanted to hear or believe.

When people in England read her book, they said,

| GUESS |

1. "How terrible!"
2. "This can't be true!"
3. "It must stop!"

The people in England said, "It can't be true."

Then Amy sent her book to government officials. They said,

1. "It can't be true!"

103

GUESS 2. "What lies!"

3. "This isn't good reading!"

The government people said, "This can't be true."

When Amy heard this, she held little Preena in her arms and cried, "Oh, God, You know these things are true. But nothing will be done because no one believes. What can I do?"

At last she saw what had to be done. "Someone must find the proof."

Amy decided

GUESS 1. it was too much for her.

2. she would prove it.

3. she had other things to do.

Amy decided, "By God's grace, I'll prove it once and for all! Someday—somehow!"

14
Proof

For three years Amy searched, but the "difficult and hard to find" facts about the temple children eluded her. She continued to care for the runaways and for a few babies left on her doorstep.

Everywhere she went with the Starry Cluster, she asked about the temple children. The Hindus

GUESS

1. didn't know about the pagans.
2. could only repeat rumors.
3. were afraid to tell.

Amy said sadly, "Rumors won't help us. And the Hindus don't know anything, or are afraid to tell."

Sometimes Amy was so tired that she felt she couldn't take another step. But she continued to work, in spite of Walker's warnings. "You will have a breakdown some day."

One day a woman sidled up to Amy and said,

GUESS

1. "I know of a temple sale."
2. "A girl is in danger."

3. "Leave here at once."

The woman said, "I know of a mother who is planning to sell her nine-year-old daughter."

"Take me to her at once!" Amy exclaimed.

The woman led the way through the crowded streets and finally pointed to a mud house. Then she disappeared.

Amy went on alone. She smiled at the woman who answered her knock, introduced herself, and told of the orphanage.

"You are too late," the woman replied. "The temple women are on their way here."

"They have not yet been paid?" Amy asked.

"No, not yet."

"Then let me take the child before they get here," Amy pleaded.

"How much do you pay?"

"Oh, I cannot *buy* children. How can that be right?" Amy struggled within herself but resisted the temptation.

The woman said, "Think about it and come back tomorrow."

Amy

GUESS	1. paid the price.
	2. went away.
	3. forgot about it.

Amy went away sorrowfully. When she came the next day, the woman told her, "I have accepted the money already." Peeking through the doorway, Amy saw

GUESS	1. the temple women.
	2. the drugged girl.
	3. a dancing child.

Amy saw the nine-year-old girl lying drugged on the floor. She shook her head and slipped down the street, where she hid behind some bushes. When she saw a cart drive up and the temple women carry the girl to the cart, she could not hold back the sobs. "Oh, Lord, help me, help me stop this!"

Her heart was weeping as she went home. She and Golden prayed and wept for hours.

"You must think of something else, Amy," Walker warned her.

So Amy dreamed of new orphanages of pretty design and lovely colors. Her dreams grew as she worked faithfully into the autumn of 1903. Then she heard that

> **GUESS**
>
> 1. Arulai's father was coming.
> 2. Ella and Mary were returning.
> 3. Walker was leaving.

To Amy's surprise Ella Crossley and Mary Hatch came to visit again. On this visit, they saw the orphanage housed in one of the old buildings left by the German count. As they walked around the compound, the friends asked, "Where did all these children come from?"

Amy said, "They are

> **GUESS**
>
> 1. temple children."
> 2. runaways."
> 3. Africans."

Amy smiled fondly. "Many of them are runaways. Children who believe in Christ and run away from the Hindu practices. Some were left here by parents. Preena, of course, is our only temple child."

"And how is Arulai?" they asked.

"She is fine. We almost lost her in a boating accident. Pearl, our one-armed woman of the Starry Cluster,

> **GUESS**
>
> 1. tipped over the raft."
> 2. saved Arulai."
> 3. drowned."

107

"A wave tipped the raft, and as Arulai was swirling into danger, the one-armed woman caught her and pulled her to safety."

"How remarkable!"

"That's not all. I feel like never letting that girl out of my sight." Amy shook her head. "Do you know that last September Arulai suffered with typhoid and pneumonia. She was at the point of death, when the nurse told me I'd have to give her up." Amy paused, remembering.

Finally, she continued. "I clung to the verse from the Bible that says, 'Blessed is the man that trusteth in Him,' and Arulai was spared once again."

Ella and Mary took pictures and made notes. "You simply must start a group to support these orphans," they urged. They visited with the Starry Cluster and talked a long time with Jewel of Life. Then they went back to England.

No sooner did Amy say good-bye, than Walker announced,

GUESS

1. "I must leave Dohnavur."
2. "Jewel of Victory is coming back."
3. "My work is done."

"Jane is seriously ill, and we must leave Dohnavur," Walker said. "But I can't leave you with the school along with your other work. I can't!"

Amy stiffened her backbone. "If you didn't go," she asked, "how could we prove that God alone is enough?"

After Walker and Jane went back to England, Amy realized that

GUESS

1. her friends were gone.
2. God alone was enough.
3. work was important.

"God alone is enough," Amy realized. "Victory is at hand. All these years I've been leaning on Walker's strength. I didn't know it, but now I know I'm totally a Jesus-walking woman. I won't even worry about the proof I need to expose the pagan temples."

God

GUESS	1. comforted her.
	2. turned her away.
	3. gave her the proof.

God comforted her, and one day He rewarded her patience.

A small orphan boy pulled at Amy's gown as she hurried from the school back to the orphanage.

"Amma."

"What is it?"

"I heard you want to know what the temple children do," he whispered.

"Yes, I need proof to put in my new book."

"Then go to the cow shed in the village and listen to the men on the other side of the wall. You will hear everything. I know because I listened myself."

"This is my chance," Amy said. She wasted no time in getting directions and preparing herself. First she

GUESS	1. covered her skin with brown stain.
	2. put on ragged clothes.
	3. wore a wig.

Amy boiled roots and made a stain for her skin. She put on a ragged sari and a cloth to cover her head. On tiptoe she crept out the door, late at night. She rode a pony to the village. Dark and menacing clouds covered the sky.

"No one even noticed me," she said, dismounting.

She slipped unnoticed into the smelly cow shed, leading her pony. Quietly she lay down beside the thin wall dividing the cow shed from the house. There she waited in the hay.

Soon four men shoved their way into the room on the other side of the wall. They had just come from the temple, and they joked about their experiences with the little temple girls.

Amy listened closely. "It makes me sick," she whispered.

When the last drunken word faded away, Amy

GUESS	1. shouted at the men.
	2. realized she now had proof.
	3. cried all the way home.

Amy rode her pony back to the orphanage. Tears streamed down her face all the way home.

"Now I know a way to get all the proof I need to convince people!"

15
Growth

Many times after listening in the cow shed that day, Amy

GUESS
1. gave up.
2. disguised herself.
3. visited the pagan temple.

Amy continued to disguise herself. She would then move silently up and down the streets looking at and listening to pagan practices. Finally she risked everything by slipping into the pagan temple itself. She watched what went on there. No one could deny what she saw with her own brown eyes. Now Amy could fight the temple customs with

GUESS
1. swords.
2. guns.
3. words.

Amy prayed for *fire words*. She told Golden, "I think the rule should be the truth, whatever people think. It is truth in a book that moves people to action."

So Amy wrote

GUESS	1. fast. 2. smoothly. 3. honestly.

She said, "Smoothness glides over souls. It does not spur them to act." Amy wrote honestly. And her new book, *Overweights of Joy,* was believed. Christians prayed. Government agents investigated. British officials found conditions as bad as Amy said. They told Amy, "If you had not proved these things, we would never have known about them. Now you can be sure we will take action to stop this abuse of children."

By June 1904, she said, "I'm responsible for seventeen children, including six saved from the temple." Twenty of the 150 Starry Cluster women

GUESS	1. cared for children. 2. visited villages. 3. planted rice.

Twenty of the Starry Cluster cared for the children, but most of them continued to give out the Word of God in the villages. They were supported by the

GUESS	1. Church of England. 2. Keswick Fellowship. 3. no one.

Those who did Christian work in the villages received help from the Church of England. But no one promised to support the orphans and their caretakers.

Amy did not believe in asking people for help. She thought it was enough to ask God alone. If supplies ran low, Amy

GUESS	1. blamed Christians.
	2. wondered how she had failed God.
	3. wondered if God was displeased with her.

Amy struggled to perfect any failures in her life, so that God could answer prayer. *I must walk with Jesus every moment!* she told herself.

One day their supply of rice was

GUESS	1. low.
	2. gone.
	3. plentiful.

The rice was gone. A merchant arrived with plenty to sell at a good price, but Amy had no money. She called the children together, and they made a circle. A Hindu playmate from the village watched what happened. While Amy and the children were praying, someone arrived with

GUESS	1. a birthday card.
	2. one hundred rupees.
	3. grain.

The one hundred rupees was enough to buy rice from the merchant. The little Hindu playmate said, "It's like the sky opened and dropped a hundred rupees from heaven."

In later years, the missionaries owned a farm where they grew their own food. One year they planted seed in October, but the weather turned hot and dry.

GUESS	1. The rice dried up.
	2. Grasshoppers came.
	3. Caterpillars hatched.

Caterpillars hatched, and Amy feared the seedlings would be

113

eaten. She called the children together, and again they prayed for God's protection. This time God sent

GUESS	1. rain. 2. birds. 3. wind.

God sent cattle egrets, which are white birds like herons. When the children came two days later, they did not find a single caterpillar. The little plants were safe.

In 1905 a welcome visitor came to Dohnavur. It was

GUESS	1. Mary. 2. Ella. 3. Amy's mother.

Amy squealed, "Oh, Mother, how glad I am to see you, after all these years!" They talked together late into the night. Mrs. Carmichael wrote home. "Amy hears the slightest cry at night from the children. She bathes, punishes, and nurses better than any mother I know."

After Mother went home, something new came to Dohnavur.

GUESS	1. The Walkers. 2. Cholera. 3. Christmas.

Walker returned with a strong, rosy Jane. But then the dread disease cholera came to Dohnavur. Jane and Amy haunted the halls of the makeshift hospital. Amy patted the backs of choking children and held their foreheads when they vomited.

"What we really need is a doctor," Amy said. She prayed for medical help as she gave out medicine and nursed the fainting children. "Oh, God, send us help." The orphanage now numbered seventy, and someone was always ill.

Amy no sooner rejoiced with six children who were baptized

than an outbreak of dysentery overtook them. When ten died, Amy cried, "I don't understand. We survived the cholera, and now—this."

Dysentery weakened the children, and they refused to eat. The days seemed like years.

Amy realized that

```
┌─────────────┐
│             │   1. the sick children should be sent away.
│    GUESS    │   2. more nurseries were needed.
│             │   3. they were overcrowded.
└─────────────┘
```

"There is no question about it. We must have medical help and more nurseries," Amy told Walker, as they sat on the veranda for a breath of air. "Golden and I have prayed and prayed."

God heard their prayers, and He sent

```
┌─────────────┐
│             │   1. Mrs. Walker.
│    GUESS    │   2. Mabel Wade.
│             │   3. Ponnammal.
└─────────────┘
```

Mabel Wade, a nurse from England, offered to come to Dohnavur. She said, "I knew, the first day, that I had come to the place God chose for me."

Amy looked into her eyes. "You offered to come, not even knowing of our desperate need. See how God answers!"

In July 1907 Amy received a letter that contained

```
┌─────────────┐
│             │   1. praise to the Lord.
│    GUESS    │   2. money for nurseries.
│             │   3. news of a death.
└─────────────┘
```

The writer said, "I want to make a gift in memory of my mother." The gift was £200, enough to build nurseries. Amy made plans for pretty buildings with lovely colors. In the years that followed, these buildings came to pass—just in time for the new babies arriving on their doorstep.

At another time a criminal came to her on his knees. "I believe he is innocent," said Amy. "I try to live at peace with all men."

Her action in helping this man, who was wanted by the police, angered a man in the village. He put up

| GUESS |

1. a loud horn.
2. a roster.
3. a loudspeaker.

The man set up a loud horn on the mud wall that surrounded the buildings of Dohnavur. All night he shouted torrents of abuse. No one could sleep. The next day he hired a gang of young men to break down the gates and wreck everything.

The Christians prayed for hours. Amy finally said, "Thank God for His protection, and go to your beds. The Lord will watch over us."

Early the next morning, the gang

| GUESS |

1. wrecked the mission.
2. tore down the wall.
3. did nothing.

For weeks everything was strangely peaceful. Then one day a Hindu woman came to the mission and said to Amy,

| GUESS |

1. "I admire you."
2. "I stopped the gang."
3. "I hate you!"

The woman said, "I overheard a gang planning to tear down the walls of the mission. I faced them. I said, 'Those people of Dohnavur worship a powerful God. When I was a child, I saw them pray for rice. At once God answered and sent a hundred rupees. I saw it myself.'"

The woman paused, and Amy waited to hear more.

116

"So I told them to be careful. I told them the Missi Ammal will not send for the police—she only needs to pray!"

"And they went away." Amy smiled, holding out her hands to the woman. "Thank you. We did pray. Wouldn't you like to know that God, too?"

16

Dohnavur Fellowship

The years passed swiftly for Amy, and changes came.

GUESS

1. Mr. Walker died.
2. Arulai died.
3. Jane went away.

Mr. Walker died, and Jane went back to England. Fortunately, an Indian worker took over the school, but Amy missed her dear friends. "Only God can comfort me at a time like this," she said.

Arulai almost died in 1915, and Amy fell to her knees beside the bed. "You know I can't bear to lose her now," she prayed. God spared the young woman, but these troubles caused Amy to lean more heavily on Jesus' strength.

"Jesus, let me walk in Your power!" she cried.

A few bright spots encouraged her.

GUESS

1. Her books were read by many.
2. Irene Streeter came to help.
3. A new boys' nursery was built.

Irene Streeter came to help, and nurseries were built in answer to prayer. The world praised Amy Carmichael, but she was too busy to notice. In Germany, she was awarded the Kaiser-in-Hind Medal for her work.

"That's nice," she agreed, "but I cannot attend the service. I have too much to do here."

During the 1920s, the compound at Dohnavur grew. Amy said, "We do need an organization

GUESS	1. to buy property."
	2. to accept money."
	3. to keep from starving."

She decided, "In order to be legal when buying property, we must have an organization." They named it the

GUESS	1. Starry Fellowship.
	2. Dohnavur Fellowship.
	3. Pride of Amy.

The Dohnavur Fellowship came into being. "I see the need!" Amy said. "Old Count Dohna did a great work here, but it shrank after he died. An organization will help to continue the work."

The work and the organization grew. God blessed with

GUESS	1. thirty-three nurseries.
	2. ten nurseries.
	3. six nurseries.

By 1923 the Fellowship operated thirty-three nurseries. Plenty of workers cared for the crowds of young children God gave to them.

In 1926 Amy prayed for a leader for the boy's work. "I also need to think of someone for leadership of the whole work," she said on her fifty-ninth birthday.

One day in 1931, Amy prayed, "Lord, do with me as Thou wilt.

Do anything, Lord!" This turned out to be a dangerous prayer answered in a strange way, for Amy

GUESS

1. died.
2. became an invalid.
3. went to America.

Late that afternoon, Amy slipped and fell as she walked across a construction site for a new building. Her back was hurt, and she became an invalid.

Now no one called her the

GUESS

1. hare.
2. Jesus-walking woman.
3. Jesus-living woman.

Now no one could call her the hare, for she didn't run, nor the Jesus-walking woman, for she didn't walk. But she was alive in Christ and lived every day for Him. When discouraged, she remembered her father's words "Never give in to difficulty." But what could she do, lying in bed all day?

She could

GUESS

1. play with the children.
2. pray with the leaders.
3. write books.

Amy was not idle the last twenty years of her life. She talked and prayed with the leaders, played with the children, and wrote thirteen more books.

By 1950 the Dohnavur Fellowship consisted of nurseries, dormitories, a school, a hospital, and a training center for Christian workers. More than two thousand people lived there.

This all came about because of the faithful work of Arulai, Preena, Jewel of Life, Golden, Mabel Wade, Irene Streeter, the Walkers, and many others, who were willing to serve God by working with the Jesus-walking woman, Amy Carmichael.

Amy died in 1951. She was eighty-four years old.

In *Ireland* Amy Carmichael, the child, wrote a poem. In *India* God made her poem come true:

> When I grow up and money have,
> I know what I will do.
> I'll build a great big lovely place
> For little girls like you.

The Dohnavur Fellowship turned out to be a "great big lovely place" for babies, little girls, little boys, young people, and the Starry Cluster of Indian women.